Crowded *with* Luck

To Fort Meyer's Friends
With aloha

Weeder

Richard Stockton Weeder, M.D. FACS

ISBN: 978-0-9777513-3-4

All sculptures by Caroline Nixon Weeder
Paintings by Juan T. Vazquez Martin
Cover design by Mercedes Soca Gil

To the women who have showed me
what it means to be a man

Erica times two, Areta, Megan, Theresa,
Mary, Lena, and Mirabai times two

Contents

Foreword

I met Richard Weeder in complete silence. We sat for a full hour, with a few dozen others at the Sarasota Quaker Meeting, in wordless worship. Afterwards, he introduced himself as "Dick Weeder from Princeton," and I felt a connection to him, because of that town which has affected both of our lives.

But if I had never met him, why would I want to read this book? The title, *Crowded with Luck*, would suggest that its author has had an extraordinarily good time in life, probably better than the lives of most of his potential readers, including me. Knowing that life is short, and that I can read only so many volumes a year, and that I'm prone to feelings of envy, why would I choose to spend precious time on Weeder's memoir?

Because I *do* know him, and because I *have* read his book, I can answer that question. I, and any reader, should come to this book not because of the success of its lucky author, but because of that author's perseverance and heart.

In my view, a better title for this work might be *Sharing the Wealth*. This collection of short memoirs (and even shorter aphorisms) reveals Dick's generosity towards his friends and family, every patient he treats, and pretty much everyone else. As interested in his friends and colleagues as he is in his own family, Dick has modeled himself on great thinkers and leaders, including one or two to whom he claims kinship.

Clearly, since adolescence he has shaped his professional and personal life with care and forethought. "Building Character" and "Savoir Faire" highlight how the maturing young man planned and worked to become the kind of person and doctor he hoped to be: ethical, hardworking, and kind. "Lucky Son" details how the elder Dr. Weeder – a renowned surgeon -- inspired his son to become an even better doctor than himself, and much of the rest of the collection reflect how he has spent his life living up to that challenge. Weeder explores both the benefits and drawbacks of competition, in sports, academics, and in medicine, showing how ultimately he came to embrace the Quaker path of seeking truth and commonality, looking for the Light within each person.

In every section, whether on music or sailing, marriage or medicine, it's clear that what the author values most, of all the valuable things he's been given and earned, is connection to other people. These snippets from the past sixty years illuminate a life that has been lucky in more ways than just material: Dick's also been lucky enough to realize how privileged his is, and not to take advantage of that privilege. From a young age into his eighties, he has held himself accountable to a high ethical standard and accepted humility in the face of inevitable change and loss.

In reflection on what he has learnt from his mentors and friends, Weeder writes: "I believe we rarely do good deeds because of demand or law, but usually because they are an outpouring of the good within us. And it is rarely because of pay: money is the lubricant of life, not the substance. Rather, spirit underlies all and is where healing and growth and imagination begin."

Weeder may have been born into privilege and had many strokes of good fortune, and thus he can call his life "crowded" with luck, but he writes with the most joy about the times that luck has been shared. His gift lies in his connection to others: his family, his friends, his colleagues, and fellow and sister Quakers. It is Dick's hope, and mine, that by perusing this chronicle from his lucky life, the reader might better feel the gift of connection, and the privilege of being together at this moment on earth, which is the luck that crowns us all.

Gillian Kendall, Ph.D.
June 2020

Acknowledgements

I've already dedicated this book to the ones I owe the most. But, to be more specific and cover some not already mentioned, let me say that Theresa Gross was most influential, by her friendship, in pulling me out of the deep hole left by the death of my wife Areta. And to Areta, I owe continued thanks for showing me the craft of writing, to such an extent as I've mastered it. Also two lovely daughters and a step-daughter, who have lovingly watched over me as I've entered a new and strange place in life. To Georgio Quochi, warm friendship through this journey as well as help in fixing up my new floating home. And to Captain Richard Correa, who has helped me keep my homes afloat and off the rocks.

To Mercedes Soca Gil, who has helped me get my intellectual, spiritual, and artistic bones moving again. She has shown me how to express myself through electronic and internet mazes which otherwise would have been impossible in this present day and (old) age.

To Helga Schwartz, Theresa Gross, and Deb Tremper, thanks for helping to get this manuscript into readable form.

To grandchildren Lena, Lucas, Mira, and Amelia, who have given me the conviction that what I leave behind will be better than I was.

Lucky Me

Only twice need a man be stiff; the
second time is when he is dead

When I was a college student, one roommate perceptively labelled me "All Business." The product of all-male schooling, I not only didn't know how to joke or have fun, I didn't know how to speak to or flirt with a girl. I even asked myself, "Are women really people?" My left leg, having once had a pulled muscle, swung stiffly in centering the ball on the soccer field. And, though I was well convinced of the benefits of yoga, my poses looked like stick figures—stiff back, stiff ideas, stiff relationships, stiff plans.

Yet now, in my eighties, I rarely complete a sentence without a pun, I tease every female I encounter, no matter how young or old. I'm interested primarily in having fun. And I'm working on an Irish brogue to accompany the blarney I'm cultivating to attract new friends. I've come to the view that the "well realized" person should be flexible, adaptable, tolerant, understanding, even funny—aware of the absurdity of life. How did I get so lucky?

I think the first stroke of good fortune happened when I was sitting in that college dorm room. Music was becoming my savior, and I'd been taking voice lessons. At this particular time, I'd taken a break from my activities as soloist in the glee club and chapel choir. And there had been a call for singers for a production of *Pirates of Penzance*. Try-outs had been running all week, and they were ending at eight o'clock. At 7:30, on a whim, I gathered some sheet music and went to the theater. The director asked what I wanted to sing for him, and I mentioned several Italian art songs and operatic arias. "Take your choice," I added. At the conclusion, the director gave me the lead. And there's where I met my wife, the daughter of a Princeton dean. She was working in the backstage crew; I was the star. She was also four years younger—still in high school. She never had a chance!

Three years later, we were married in the chapel by another dean. Then we had many wonderful years together and two lovely daughters, the prides of my life.

Comment:

The greatest fun I ever had, before or since, had been courting, playing with, and winning Erica. It lasted until the Medical Dean at Penn said, "Marry that girl, and get back to work."

Caruso and Me

Practicing the piano was boring. As much as I liked music and appreciated concerts, particularly in the seat at the Academy of Music close to Dad, I liked it best when I heard him nicely play Saint Saens, Rachmaninoff, and Chopin on our old Steinway. Music spoke a noble language, a speech with infinite messages, and moods often reflecting my own. But even after seven years, piano was not for me.

My least favorite genre was opera. Despite the fact that Dad's mother was a professional singer of great talent, I just "didn't get it." Singing didn't appeal until, lazy me, I found out that you *couldn't* practice with the voice more than a few minutes a day. And your instrument was always handy, so it didn't require a truck and moving men to concertise with your favorite sounding board at a far distance. And then, only you knew when you screwed up badly, with wrong keys or a forgotten phrase. Or, at least, not as obvious. These were the great advantages of a voice as musical instrument.

So I gave it a try. And, as I did, I became aware of the difficulty of sound production from the lungs, vocal chords, and bony mask of a face. I began to glory in the uniquely personal and chocolatey rich sounds the talented singer could produce. The shading of tone and alteration of sentiment was more imitated than matched by orchestral instruments. I was blessed with a fairly good light baritone capable of being "pushed up" into tenor with practice, good breath support, and courage. Increasingly, I was given tenor parts in my high school chorus, and with that prominence gained the presidency of the club and respect of my schoolmates.

Then, one fateful day, my voice teacher asked me to sing for someone. Not a concert or recital, this was to be a private trial, with no audience to giggle or applaud. My audience of one was the distinguished and lovely first harpist of the Philadelphia Orchestra, first chair since she was sixteen. Mrs. Samuel Rosenbaum, mother of one of my fellow students, played under her maiden name, Edna Phillips.

The three of us met in the music room. Mr. Finch, my teacher, accompanied me as I sang a couple of Italian and French art songs. Then he launched into the *pièce de résistance*, an operatic aria of love between a simple young farmer and his more wealthy and sophisticated long-time neighbor. The song relates the story: the ardent swain has bought a love potion to win his pretty love, but to no avail—she seems partial to a dashing soldier. Distraught, he confronts her. Telling of his heartache he suddenly sees in the woman's eye, "a furtive tear." The aria dominates and wraps up "A Love Potion," by Gaetano Donizetti.

So, with fear and trepidation, I began. Facing few soaring high notes, I managed to portray what I knew of youthful ardor. And Mr. Finch and I landed in the same key at the same time. Miraculous!

Miss Philipps then remarked generously, "That was very nice, Dick. Reminds me of when I accompanied Caruso on the harp for his recording of this aria at RCA."

Shocked, I blurted out, "That's the last time I sing for you, Miss. Philips." And so it was.

Comment:

My brother Dana and I were both fierce competitors and best friends, as only brothers can be. But I had followed him, like a puppy dog, through all of our growing up—school, college, medical school, and career choice. We parted company only after our very different experiences with the Vietnam War. But at the time of this story, we were in college together. He had proceeded me as a good student, with all the right school activities and three sports. But his record had been slightly better; instead of varsity soccer in school, he had captained his team. Instead of just being on the tennis team, he had been Middle States doubles champ. Instead of his getting a "letter" on the varsity soccer team at Princeton, I only played the occasional game. But as far as music was concerned, he had participated where I had stood out. In the family, and those who knew us, it was my "claim to fame." But, more important, I felt myself capable of success out of the shadow of my kin.

The Sound of My Voice

I have to face it—I'm a ham. And the pleasure in performing has seeped, like a stain, through to one of my daughters and to a granddaughter, who will dance with swooping arms and gauze cloth at the least invitation.

In my daughter's case, it has been an advantage, as she performs with her violin "at the top of her game," as compared with most who struggle to do as well in performance as in rehearsal.

But what a great time I had at Princeton, in two different singing groups, and the opera where I "snowed" the lovely woman who would become my wife and the mother of my children. Beside the weekly performances of sacred works in the chapel, the more occasional glee club concerts, complete with sea-shanties and football-fight songs, there were a few outstanding occasions. The evening get-together with a pianist who would become the accompanist for Sherril Milnes, the baritone star of the Metropolitan Opera. I think I reached an E above high C that night for the only time in my life. Or the time I walked into my teacher's studio and she introduced me to my accompanist of the day, the world-famous harpsichordist Ralph Kirkpatrick. He'd stopped by for a visit with his old friend, my teacher.

I'm not proud of the day when I was scheduled to solo in a joint "football concert" with Harvard. It was "houseparties weekend," and I had eagerly anticipated my date's arrival. Prior to the evening, I had gone out looking for a room for her to stay.

She was a nice woman. My father had dated her mother, the daughter of the U.S. ambassador to France, during his army days in France. But I had been looking for something a bit less expensive than "the Nass" (Nassau Inn), which was beyond my budget. I had found a nice house on Bayard Lane that let rooms for college dates, which I eventually took. I also stopped into Mrs. Bloomer's big old square Victorian on Mercer Street. Above the long center hall staircase, the second-floor rooms circled around the circumference of the great expanse below. Each room lacked a door, but had in its place a curtain. Inside each was a washstand, with big bowl and water pitcher. There was a triangular Princeton banner in each room, with the date "77." But this was still 1954!

I retreated down the stairs and met Mrs. Bloomer at the door. I was somewhat nonplussed by the fact that she had only one functional eye. But when I glanced out the glass front door, what should I notice but Albert Einstein strolling by on the arm of his niece. It struck me that I had witnessed the Victorian age, the modern age, and the atomic age, all in one afternoon. But that's Princeton.

But back to houseparties. My date had called and said she would be very late, much too late to hear me solo at the concert. I was pissed. So, what did I do? I went down Prospect Street to my eating club and got pissed. I think I polished off five whiskey sours. By concert time, I was none too steady on my feet. But I got to Alexander Hall, stood up at the opening chords, and sang

"The Song of the Birds" as well as ever. Only problem was the next day when a friend asked why I had been swaying so much during my solo, presumably in time to the music.

The most fabulous experience, however, was not at college. My old teacher at high school was conducting a performance of the Mozart Requiem in Philadelphia,. and asked me to do the tenor solo, for which I would be paid. I jumped at the chance. The concert came off as scheduled, and I guess I did O.K. But what really delighted me was to drive back to college, gather my roommates together, and listen to the recorded performance on the radio.

Comment:

Though probably headed into medicine, this gave me a viable option. I carried more than one arrow in my quiver.

With a Little Luck from My Giraffe

Mother was a fine sculptor, throwing up good heads of most of us, a great one of dad. But her most interesting project was to do portraits of nine animals so that blind students could understand what they would never see. Done to scale, for the reasons of comparison, they were little "works of art," and, incredibly, predicted my daughter Erica's monuments on the roofs of Disney's hotels in Orlando. But that's another story.

My story began one evening when mother came back despondent from her sculpting day at the Philadelphia Zoo. At dinner, she hardly spoke. It was obvious something was amiss.

"What's wrong, mom," I asked, over the soup.

"My giraffe died," mom replied.

"Well, that's terrible. Can you finish the piece?"

"Yes. It was very sudden, but I think I have enough to do a good likeness."

The next morning at Penn (I was living at home during my first year at med school), I had my least favorite subject—pathology. I hiked the distance from the local train, walking alongside one of my favorite professors, Johnathan E. Roades, later to be one of my (and Penn's) Quaker heroes.

With trepidation, I entered the path lab to find Dr. Ratcliff holding a steel basin with a large fresh heart within.

"Gentlemen," (it should have been, 'and ladies') "take a look at this. What do you see."

"Well," said one of my colleagues, "It's a large heart, thick muscles."

"Yes," said Ratcliff. "Does anyone know where this heart may have come from?"

I, knowing that Ratcliff also served the zoo, knew where.

Drawing myself up to my most intelligent height, I proclaimed, "Looks like a giraffe heart to me."

Indeed, there lay mother's model.

Ratcliff looked at me with amazement. And that's how I passed pathology. I never let on how I knew. I'd learned by then not to look a gift horse in the mouth. Or, for that matter, a gift giraffe's.

Battling Elephants

Mom's visits to the zoo to sculpt animals for the students at the Philadelphia School for the Blind were sometimes dramatic. One model, Josephine the elephant, was a favorite, and she seemed to have a sweet disposition. The sculpture was fine art.

But Josephine's cage-mate, Cleopatra, was well named after the warlike and seductive Queen of Egypt. One evening at dinner, I got the picture, because Mom smelled awful. She usually had a lovely odor of Chanel number five, and washed regularly. I know—she impressed regular bathing on me since my days as a rough and tumbling teenager. But this evening she smelled more than foul. "What gives?" I thought.

Well, that morning she had been working on Josephine, who was calmly munching in her cage. Sneakily, Cleo started wandering around the shared cage, snuffing noisily through her trunk. One side, then the other, a gigantic living vacuum cleaner, sniffing up the detritus, foul debris, and unmentionable until she had a trunkful. Turns out, in typical female fashion, she was jealous of the attention her cage-mate was receiving. Was Josephine younger, or had she a better elephant build? You'd have to ask Cleo. But what was a queen royal to do, but blast the foul snootfull in her trunk in Mom's direction, covering her with foulness?

Being an intelligent species, I guess jealousy is also a part of the elephant's emotional vocabulary.

But from then on, Mom wore a very smelly old coat on her visits to her animal models. I was grateful, and had a better appetite for dinner.

Lucky Son

My father was bigger than life, the only person I knew who, on entering a room, would draw everyone's eyes onto himself. Handsome, yes, solid, yes, eloquent, yes. Put a cap on him and he'd be the "very model of the modern Major General." I've spent my life puffing myself up to his stature.

Yet one day, he sat me down and told me that I would be a better surgeon than he. It's the only thing he ever said to me that I didn't believe. But what sweet kindness! And what a legacy to give a highly competitive young man in the same profession! More than I can say, I miss his dignified nobility even after forty years. He was a worthy descendent of our Plantagenet ancestry.

He was born poor—but his opera-singing mother's voice put him through medical school after he'd spent only two and a half years in high school, no college. He grew a mustache to look older, joined the army, and went to war-weary France as "Surgeon to the Supreme War Council," treating the Secretary of War, as he was titled then. How could this be? Dad's father had sold women's stockings door-to-door to assist in supporting the family, a man as quiet as his wife was expressive.

My father's secret was this—his mother adored him. She set him on such a high pedestal, it left him no possibility of failure.

When Dad returned to Penn after the war, he taught anatomy to the students. They gave him a nickname, "The Prince of Wales." Many years later, he gave anatomy demonstrations to me and my classmates, setting up a blackboard in our living room. Not only did he know his anatomy cold, he could draw, which was well beyond me.

Dad's most winning characteristic was his sense of humor. A fierce, clenched-lips competitor, he demonstrated his skill on the squash court with a deadly backhand. One unlucky player discovered this when he crowded my father one too many times. Dad then took a full swing and broke his squash racket on the offending backside. My father then gleefully told me that, in the shower, his rival looked as if he'd sat down on a steaming waffle iron.

Sometimes my father considered himself a knight in shining armor, or more exactly a Buick, when charging down the streets of Philadelphia. Coming back home one day through Fairmont Park, Dad got himself into a Le Mans mood and wheeled back and forth on the torturous route, one too many times cutting off a Chrysler. Then he and the Chrysler came to a side by side stop at the long light at Ridge Avenue. The Chrysler, on the left, reached across his wife's seat and cranked the window down. And so followed an invective insulting equally to both my father's driving and his ancestry. Dad, his intervening window also open, waited, nodding, until the long light greened, then leaned over to ask the wife, "Is he like this in the home too?" followed by a heavy foot on the accelerator, squealing rubber, and a giggling wife.

Dad's greatest joy was trading pomposity with the lawyers downtown. One case stands out. Dad had been referred an elderly lady with intestinal obstruction, frail to the point of severe dehydration. With her too sick for surgery, Dad ordered intravenous fluids, but to no avail. On the patient's death, my father found that the young couple who had cared for his patient had sneakily brought in a lawyer to draw up a deathbed will. The case went to court on the out-of-town niece's demand. The contest became interesting when my father testified that, when the new will had been written, the patient was delusional and hallucinating, incontinent in the bed.

The lawyer drew up to his full height, hooked his thumbs under his vest, and leaned forward to interrogate Dad.

"Dr. Weeder, you have been qualified to testify as an expert witness in surgery, is that not correct?"

"Yes."

"And yet you are testifying as to the mental capacity of the patient. Is that not the province of a psychiatrist?"

My father leaned forward in the witness box, hooked his thumbs under his vest, looked the lawyer in the eye, and responded, "when a doctor refers me a patient, I accept the head along with the body."

The judge bent over his bench. "You have no more questions for Dr. Weeder, do you, Mr. Counselor?"

How can a son not adore a father like that?

My father's first assistant in raising me was the club. My grandparents lived in Chestnut Hill, on a dignified suburban street. At the back of their garden was a gate which opened onto the grounds of the Philadelphia Cricket Club, so old and hoary that the members no longer played cricket, but rather tennis, squash, and nine holes of golf. The centerpiece of the grounds, away from the nine holes, was a gigantic square of tennis courts, seven courts by seven, or forty-nine in total. Reigning over this magnificent lawn was the squash and tennis pro Jimmy Reed. He and dad had together designed the four squash courts, three singles and one double, the best courts in Philadelphia. The tennis courts, not to be outdone, hosted the U.S. Open Tennis tournaments. From them, as a ball boy, I witnessed up close the great Pancho Gonzales, equally talented Pancho Segura, and skillful Vic Seixas. My pay was in used balls, hot off the court, and the best iced tea I'd ever drunk.

But the pro's friendship with dad went much deeper. One day he showed up with a spot on his lung. The diagnosis was obvious—he'd been a heavy smoker, even as a professional athlete. He appealed to Dad. He needed to have his lung out, and he wanted my father to do it.

No surgeon in Philadelphia had yet removed a lung. But Dad's operative field was "the skin and its contents." So, in his thoroughness, competence, and large ego, he took it on. Having taught anatomy at Penn for ten years, he still went back to the morgue and dissected a few cadavers to refresh his memory. Then he operated on Jimmie who, with such good general fitness, sailed through surgery and went home. But neither Jimmie nor Dad was finished. The club directors decided that Jimmie's limited wind kept him from returning to his place as tennis pro, so he was made head groundskeeper over the magnificent square of tennis courts.

Meanwhile I, an avid though mediocre athlete, played my heart out on the tennis courts in the summer, and scuffed them up in the fall on the club soccer team. Then, struggling mightily to grow a croquet court on our small lawn back home, I applied to Jimmie.

"How is it possible, Jimmie, to keep this tennis lawn so fine when we soccer players are digging divots out every fall?"

"The secret is this, Dick. The foundation of this lawn, built over a hundred years ago, goes down four feet. About a foot of heavy stone, another of light stone, then another of gravel, sand, loam, and rich topsoil. That's how it's done."

About the same amount of knowledge, planning, skill and care as Dad had put into Jimmie's surgery.

My relationship to Dad was best expressed one day when, after I don't remember what teenage-male thing I'd done, he sat me down and said the following. "Dick, I want you to know that, no matter what you ever say or do, I will always love you." And that pretty well sums up the difference between liking someone and loving. You might disagree with what is said to you, but if the relationship is just "like," you will tell the person, at least in your mind, to get lost, or jump in the lake. But if you love, you take a deep breath and keep loving them the same as before.

Geisinger Days

I'd been around Penn enough to see the way the surgical residency worked there. It was a superlative program, but it prepared the graduates for mostly academic careers, which was not where I wanted to end up. And I'd seen the program my father provided at Germantown Hospital, which my brother was taking. It seemed to me that here at least, I should have a different viewpoint than following in his footsteps, as I had before. I did take my internship at Germantown, and it was a valuable experience.

So I went down to Penn and talked to I.S. Ravdin, the chairman of Penn's department of surgery. One of the country's leading surgical educators, he had served as President of the American College of Surgeons, and had operated on President Eisenhower. He would know how to steer me in the direction I wanted to go. I told him I wanted to start operating as soon as possible, under supervision, of course. He suggested two places, the Guthrie Clinic in Sayre, Pennsylvania, and the Geisinger Clinic in Danville. After visiting both, I chose the latter.

Geisinger had been started after Abigail Geisinger decided to do something to honor her husband. She had chosen one of Will Mayo's first assistants, Harold Foss, to be the first physician and surgeon. Good choice, as Foss was a man of superb organizational skills, complete integrity, and vision. The place thrived. The only glitch occurred when Mrs. Geisinger named the "ministers of the town" to act as the Board of Trustees. The small town of Danville had two ministers of each denomination: two Presbyterian, two Lutheran, two Baptist, two Episcopalian—you get the picture. Only one Catholic, of course. The thing came to a head one day when Dr. Foss found the ministers making rounds on the hospital floors, and suggesting treatment. Foss gave Abigail a choice: Either the ministers cleared out, or he did.

From then on, his word was law, and he ran a tight ship—in more ways than one. He decided to take up sailing, and bought for his first boat a sixty-five-foot schooner, kept at Martha's Vineyard. Also took up flying, and had thirteen planes until he cracked one up, and it ended up being paraded through town on the back of a truck. Then everyone in town learned than his great surgical skills did not extend to the controls of a plane.

He was elected to American surgery's highest office, the presidency of the American College of Surgeons. He stood out here too. There was at the time a shameful focus of corruption in American medicine—the practice of fee-splitting. By this arrangement, a surgeon who'd been referred a patient would split his operative fee with the family doctor who'd sent him the case. This meant, of course, that the surgeon chosen was not necessarily the best available, but the one willing to give the largest kickback to the referring doc. Harold Foss ended fee-splitting with a single blow: any surgeon caught sharing his fee was out of the college—immediately. This corruption became a thing of the past, and patients benefitted.

When I got to Geisinger, Doctor Foss had been long retired, but his home was still on the hospital campus. He, of course, had known Dad. So it was natural that the evening my parents visited, the Fosses came to dinner. Awkwardly, I got out slides of Erica's and my honeymoon trip to Europe. Dr. Foss carefully corrected me when I mistakenly identified a European cathedral. The breadth of the man's knowledge was extraordinary.

I thrived at Geisinger. Always a tinkerer, I thought to build a machine to control bleeding in the stomach of patients with a gastric ulcer. They gave me an unused old operating room for my workshop, and I fashioned a simple but effective apparatus to cool the stomach. It both cut down on the blood flow to the organ and decreased the acid level. There was on the market a very expensive cooling gadget, but mine cost practically nothing and worked just as well. We used it in the Intensive Care Unit, and I wrote it up for the local medical journal.

Then I got involved in the care of burns with Dr. Frank Gerow, who had, as a resident, devised the silicon breast prosthesis. We used a silicon fluid bath for long-term debridement of the most severe burns, and published our results in *The Journal of the Society of Plastic and Reconstructive Surgery*. Generously, the authors chose me to present the paper at the annual meeting of the Society in Las Vegas.

My presentation was the same day that my father suddenly dropped dead. I've never liked Las Vegas since then, despite the honor.

But the biggest honor was toward the end of my residency when Dr. Foss asked me and Erica to be his guests in Florida at a meeting of the Southern Surgical Society, the most prestigious surgical group in the country. Dr. and Mrs. Foss had a cottage at Boca Raton, the site of the meeting, but elected to stay in the hotel where the meeting took place. We would occupy the cottage.

I don't remember how Erica occupied her time, I was in a daze, in the center of the cream of American surgery. Dr. Foss introduced me to every one, Debakey and Cooley of Houston, Howard Patterson of New York… I can't now remember them all. We had dinner with the Ochsners, Dr. and Mrs. Alton, and their son John. Dr. Ochsner told me how the family had gotten their name—by castrating bulls to make them into oxen. He also mentioned his descent from Paracelsus, the father of modern medicine. And he told me how he had trained Michael Debakey. When I remarked that I'd heard that Debakey only slept two hours a night, Ochsner noted that his habit was the same.

When Erica and I boarded the train back to Danville, I thought I'd spent the weekend in Valhalla!

Comment:

I never heard that Foss had treated any other resident as he had me. He'd put me on a pedestal, much as grandmother had my father. From then on, I felt that anything was possible. My reach had increased.

Captured

The situation was this: I had finished my surgical residency and travelled to Japan to fulfill my obligation to the Army Medical Corps. I would be caring for soldiers injured in Viet Nam who'd been sent to one of our three hospitals there. Four weeks after I'd arrived, Erica and our two-year-old daughter, Cricket, joined me. Prior to their arrival, I had rented a typical Japanese home, "on the economy," as base housing was full. I'd sat in the little house, with tatami mat floors, shoji rice-paper walls, and a drum of kerosene outside, and signed a lease with my landlord, a general in the Japanese army. I had the forethought to ask him where we might find babysitters while Erica and I explored the wonders and fun of downtown Tokyo. He had said there was a school which taught English to young women "over there," as he vaguely gestured with his hand.

The night in question, Erica, Cricket and I squeezed into our two-seater Honda convertible in search of the school. We'd headed "over there," and soon found a large complex surrounded by a high concrete wall complete with iron gate. The gate being open, I drove in.

The students inside were not girls, but young men. They were oriental, all right, but nothing I heard sounded like Japanese. Certainly not English. One did speak accented English.

"Who are you?" he said, and I smiled—he didn't even try.

"I'm an American, a doctor."

"Why are you here?"

"I'm in the army, treating wounded soldiers."

"Come with me." A group of other hostiles around him made the invitation appear less than cordial.

Leaving my precious ones in the car, I entered a windowless, rectangular room with some twenty other grim faces.

"Who are you?," again.

Same reply.

"And what are you doing here?"

Same reply.

"And what is the United States doing in this part of the world?"

That's a good question. What right had the United States military to be half way around the world? And to be killing men, women, and children they'd never met?" And why was I, a supposed healer, participating in butchery? It was an existential question for me, for my partners, for my president, for those friends who had voted for him. What right had we to impose our ideas, our bullets, our bombs, on a society which was attempting to make sense of the place and time where they lived, far from the good old U.S.?

The questions continued for, I suppose, hours, with my dear ones patient in the Honda outside. Then it came to a climax. "Does any one know you are here?"

"Yes," I said—a half-truth.

"Who is that?'

"My landlord."

"And who is he?"

"A general in the Japanese army" A whole truth.

The leader paused a moment, glanced at another, then got up, led me to the door, and motioned me to my car. The gate clanged open as I accelerated in reverse.

The next morning, Military Intelligence debriefed me, informing me that, without that extraordinary good luck, my family and I could simply have disappeared, perhaps in two and a half weighted bags in the bottom of Tokyo bay. We'd wandered into a North Korean University! The Japanese government had granted this university the political and legal autonomy of an embassy. The Japanese police never set foot on North Korean universities, to say nothing of our U.S. Army.

Of course, right after we'd escaped the compound, we frantically fled our mat and paper dollhouse, with its highly flammable kerosene tank just outside the back door.

Comment:

I think this is the moment when I parted company from my brother, and grew in a different direction. At this point, he remained adherent to the authority around him, feeling the Vietnam conflict was a proper activity for our nation. This point of view remained with him to his death, and it continued a painful separation for us both. Even in his last, failing days, my intimate nursing of him failed to fully bridge the gap. We remained separate as I and his wife watched him take his last breath.

Jackie's Bikini

Having just been discharged from the army medical corps, and returned from Japan, I was still in an order-receptive mood. So when the call came in at lunch in Hyannisport that Bobby Kennedy needed a crew for the race that afternoon, I saluted and volunteered for the duty.

We didn't do very well. The rest of the crew was Bobbie's son and a local politico, who spoke politics on both windward and leeward legs. I was to set the spinnaker—Bobbie didn't know I had been third mate on Dad's boat, so either my sister or brother had been the experts on setting that sail. All things considered, neither the Kennedy competitiveness nor the Weeder competitiveness were well served that race. And when the time came for me to pick up the mooring buoy, I fell into the water. What a performance!

But Bobby, with his typical grace, still asked me to come back to the compound for a drink, even though I was soaking wet. It turned into a special occasion. I luckily fell into conversation with Jackie Kennedy. I drank in her charm with the vodka tonic. She was all I'd heard her to be.

That night in bed, as Erica and I laid down the happenings of the day, I asked her, "Did Jackie Kennedy have a Caesarean section?"

Erica, suddenly upright in bed," Did you see Jackie Kennedy?"

"Of course. I had a drink with her. She was very nice."

"And what about the C. section?"

"Well, she was in a bikini. Had a large scar on her belly."

"You saw Jackie Kennedy in a bikini, and you didn't tell me about it?"

The wifely curiosity must have imagined Jackie and me in bed together. It was several days before I could get her settled down again.

Savoire Faire

Surgery is a craft, and those who don't appreciate the fact will never make good surgeons. I've often envisioned myself standing on the shoulders of the craftsmen who went before me, up to and including my father. Surgical journals are full of articles which describe a technical trick such as how to use a specific instrument, how to close a particular wound. The tradition was for surgeons to invent both instruments and techniques, labeling them with their names, and thus obtaining a sort of immortality. The Deaver was a retractor, invented by my father's hero and the grandfather of a friend. The Foss retractor was devised by my old chief at Geisinger, where I trained. Whipple, of the Whipple operation, was my premedical advisor after he left Columbia. It was the golden age of surgery where one man could hope, with energy and cleverness, to single-handedly save many a life, devise new techniques, and leave a legacy of legend. And I was lucky enough to meet and know many of these innovators.

No credit to me. I just happened to be there, and it was a closely knit brotherhood, international in scope. Sir James Patterson Ross, a relative of my wife at the time, operated on King George; he was also a friend of Foss and my father. I saw him at St. Barts, in London, where I took a clerkship. Francis Moore of Harvard was examined for his Surgical Boards by my dad and Whipple. He was also father-in-law of my brother's surgical partner. Loyal Davis, professor in Chicago, I met at a surgical meeting. He was Reagan's father-in-law, and Davis's son, at Penn, one of my teachers. DeBakey, father of vascular surgery, examined me for my Boards. I came into contact with Cooley, the magician of Houston, and Ochsner of the Ochsner Clinic. Ravdin, Eisenhower's surgeon, Rhoads, and Johnson were all at Penn. C. Everett Koop taught me at Children's and later became Surgeon General under Reagan.

All these men inspired me, passing on their trade secrets with a full hand, whether in person or in the literature. Nobody was patenting procedures or instruments to make a profit. The idea was to serve the public by making your students as good as possible. Give them all the tools at your disposal, and their skill was your reward, their glory reflected back to you. Surgery was a guild, in the best sense of the term.

I remember a surgical meeting one morning at Geisinger. There were about six papers on the program; I had one, as chief resident, on a project I'd been pursuing. But the star of the morning was Admiral Brown, Surgeon General of the Navy (Imagine that, an admiral that cut people instead of waves, and a general as well as admiral!). But Admiral Brown's talk was on gall bladder surgery, and he described a trick for exploring the common bile duct that he'd learned from my father. Talk about full circle, and small world.

The technique described by the admiral from my father involved a fundamental rule of manual labor: your hand must be comfortable to do its best work. Most people explore the common duct from the right side of the operating table, inserting their hand around the "portal triad" and feeling the structures with the finger tips. This is awkward as it involves hyperextending the left hand, if you use that one, or turning the right hand upside-down, equally awkward. My dad's idea was to move to the other side of the operating table, insert the left hand, and grasp the structures in a comfortable position, with full sensitivity of feeling. It reminds me of how my daughter was trained to position her hands accurately but comfortably when she first learned the violin, and of how I was trained to hold the hands as they lay on the piano keys. And so it is with other surgical techniques: how to hold a scissors or hemostat, how to examine a thyroid or breast. The hand must be in a comfortable, neutral position to do its most sensitive work.

Yet this is not the only way to learn. One can also learn from those who are not so admirable. There was one surgeon on my service in the army who evoked little respect from any of us. He was lazy, uncaring and self-centered. But he had a very good trick to teach about wound care. And one resident I knew stated that he was tempted at the end of his service to thank an inept chief for all the lessons he'd learned from the chief's mistakes. Yet this older man must have had some talent to inspire patient loyalty, at least. One of his patients returned to him seven times to have the same hernia repaired.

I hate to think of what would happen if this tradition of learning through mentoring were to disappear from surgical training, replaced by textbooks and computer programs. Not only would young surgeons have to reinvent the simplest hand-skills, but the spirit of dedication and colleagueality would be lost. The surgeon, while seemingly a confident, even egotistical, craftsman, is in reality dependent for spiritual nurturing on patients, colleagues, and staff. Once "rattled" in the operating room, a surgeon becomes inept and unsure, a participant in disaster.

The staff, particularly the nurses and assistants, are constantly boosting the surgeon's ego, expressing their confidence in him and in the outcome. During a difficult case, petty animosities and competition are banished for the sake of the patient's survival. Of even greater importance is the feeling that one is supported by a legion of those who have gone before, who survived similar crises, developed the tools to deal with them, and passed those tools along.

To go even deeper, not all knowledge is learned. I appreciated that fact when I became son-in-law to one of Princeton's many physicists and Nobel laureates. This man was an original, like no one else, his discoveries highly individualistic. Originally a chemist, the only physics courses he ever attended were those he taught. One day I asked him where his best ideas came from. He answered, not in the laboratory, not during study, but from "out of the blue," during long walks. He was inspired in the literal meaning of the term; he breathed in, as it were, his discoveries. An undeniable genius, his scientific method was closer to art than craft, more creation than unearthing. Like others of this rare type, he did original things because he hadn't been taught that they couldn't be done. But he was not like most of us.

So I am grateful for my mentors, my predecessors in surgery. I bless them for skill, for inventiveness, for courage to dare new things. Most of all, I bless them for the generosity of spirit to pass on their skills to us who stand on their shoulders. That spirit makes it possible for us to reach higher than they did. And our patients are the beneficiaries. My father, in the kindest thing he ever said to me, predicted that I would be a better surgeon than he. If I was, it was only because I was standing on his shoulders.

Lucky Dad

Nixon had just resigned. Our three medical families, vacationing together on Prince Edward Island, had seen his scowling, lying, face on the only television one of our cottages provided. The next morning, as usual, we'd packed up picnics, towels, and life-rings, and made our way off the plane of the island, down the steep thirty-foot slope onto the beach. Three doctor friends, our wives, and assorted kids. I was carrying four-month-old Megan in her car-bed—nine-year-old Cricket and Erica led the way.

We got to the bottom and I wearily set the car bed down, thinking, 'This kid is getting too heavy.' We were about twenty feet from the steep, almost cliff-like, slope above the sandy beach.

Then Cricket piped up, "No, Dad, put Megan down closer to the water."

"Why, Kid? This place is fine," I replied

"Because the cliff might collapse."

'What a stupid idea,' I thought. 'But hell, I'll humor her. Easier than arguing.' So I moved Megan in her bed forty feet closer to the water.

About thirty minutes later, the bluff did collapse, rolling boulders to where Megan had been lying.

* * *

"There are more things under heaven and earth, Horatio, than are known in your philosophy."

* * *

Needless to say, my daughters are very close, the one always aware of the existential debt she owes the other. Their mother, Erica, step-mother Areta, and I always rejoiced in the girls' relationship. But beware of the explosion of talents you may turn loose with your procreation. Keeping up with these two has been a never-ending uphill climb. I'm getting tired, even as I smile.

Cricket (Erica) as an architectural student had followed the request of her mentor, Michael Graves, and mimicked the talents of her two sculptor grandmothers to render two forty-five-foot swans for the top of Disney's Orlando Hotel. These swans are, together with two dolphins on the Dolphin Hotel, seen daily by more vacationers than ever saw me on Oprah.

And Megan, playing violin with John Mellancamp at Rockefeller Center, Sean Lennon on Letterman's show, and Natalie Merchant at the Royal Albert Hall, has played more sweet sounds than were ever read in my books. My God, how lucky can one father be?

Comment:

I need to say more about this. That Cricket had predicted the falling cliff was not just she felt it better to be closer to the

shore, or that she had heard before that the cliffs occasionally slid down (which she had not), or that I had humored this nine-year-old offspring's whim, which I usually would not have. All rather unusual. Was this some sort of telepathy from the future?

A group of us were talking about this the other day, and each described one or more experiences that defied logic, an uncanny prediction, a visitation from the past, or whatever. Indeed, who has not had such an inexplicable happening in their life, a one in a million coincidence? It brings into question the limits of human intelligence. Shakespeare noted it, as usual. And it posits, once again, the great unknowable beyond.

Shooting The Star

I was awakened about midnight that Sunday night by a call from the emergency room. The patient was a sixteen-year-old boy, injured earlier that day in a league soccer match. There was a question of a ruptured spleen with internal bleeding, and his blood pressure was dropping. I dressed hurriedly and climbed into the car.

The drive to the hospital was filled with memories of the game. I'd played soccer from before high school, through college, into medical school, when I played in an interclub league in Philadelphia, I was never that good—played college soccer, but never got a varsity letter. The inter-club soccer exposed me to All-Americans, a few on each of the club teams. I was good enough to know the sport well, and to love it. I loved the competition, and the challenge of tackling a good player. I loved the teamwork of intricate passing patterns down to the opposing goal. I loved, in a word, the possibility of both starring and of being a member of a team, the interplay between egotism and submission to the group good.

I loved the exertion of taking the ball at maximum speed down my side of the field, and I loved the leisure of wandering around watching play on the other side. I enjoyed challenging the opposing player with the ball, and trying to evade him when I was in possession. I loved controlling my body as I did the ball. And, of course, I loved taking a shot on goal, a chance to be a hero. Those were rare moments, sweeter for their rarity!

I loved the feeling at the end of the game, the long, hot shower, snacking on cookies and cider in the clubhouse, reliving the scores and the good plays with the players from both teams. I felt soft energy and sweet fatigue in my body, fully alive, an athlete, and very much a man. At the end of a good game, I felt ready for anything life might bring. And if the play had been hard but fair, I was a brother of every player.

Arrival at the hospital, guided by twenty years of daily commute, brought me back to the night. Adrenalin was starting to banish sleepiness, with the thought that a life was waiting to be saved, or a surgical reputation ready to be tarnished, as the case might be. I climbed out of the car, and entered the emergency room. The boy was lying on a stretcher, pale and drawn, surrounded by parents and a sibling. The C.T. scan was on the view box, read by the radiologist as showing a damaged spleen and free fluid in the belly. The "free fluid," of course, was blood. The boy's pulse was up, his blood pressure slightly down. The safest course was to operate.

There was a choice. I could wait and "observe" the patient—see if his blood pressure, pulse, and blood count remained stable, evidence that his internal bleeding had stopped. There were articles in the literature supporting such a choice. But, in a sense, he had already been observed, as the injury had taken place early in the afternoon. After the initial pain of the blow, he had seemed to stabilize, felt better, and had gone home to his family. It was only after he had felt worse, and faint, that he was taken to the

E.R. and evaluated. So, chances were, he was still bleeding. I asked about the injury.

The soccer player (I'll call him Jerry) was one of the stars of his team, a high scorer. He'd been handling the ball along the side line when an opposing player decided to attack him, and seemed to go after him rather than the ball, according to the witnesses. In any case, the opposing player kicked Jerry in the stomach, rupturing his spleen. The motivation seemed proven by the fact that the opposing team had taunted Jerry as he lay in pain on the field, laughing at his injury.

When I heard the story, I was crushed. It was the opposite of the feeling that I'd had about the sport. I'd always felt that soccer was a better game than football or ice hockey because good sportsmanship played such a large part. The focus was always on improving one's skills rather than winning by cheating or by injuring an opponent. But there was no time to dwell on feelings now, a decision had to be made or the situation might end in tragedy. I called my partner, waking him from a sound sleep.

The way it worked was this: for most cases, we used the residents to assist. But with spleen or liver injuries, or major colon cases, another skilled pair of hands was sometimes needed. A few moments lost at a crucial point could make a difference between survival and disaster. So I made the call. Besides, my partner had played soccer too. He would sympathize with my feelings.

The patient was brought quickly to the operating room, prepared, and anesthetized. Technically, he was a pleasure to operate on—thin but muscular, no fat blocking the way, and in excellent physiological shape to withstand both surgery and anesthesia. I swiftly made the incision, cauterized the bleeders, and, with one hand, retracted the stomach and colon out of the way. The spleen was, as suggested by the C.T. scan, lying in two halves on a pool of blood. We sucked out the blood and cleaned up. The spleen continued oozing blood, leaving me a second decision.

The quickest, easiest and short-term safest procedure was to remove both halves of the spleen. We would all be back home in bed within an hour. But total removal of the organ would leave Jerry at increased risk for overwhelming infection from loss of the immune function which the spleen provides, particularly in youngsters. Repairing all or part of the organ would be a better long-term treatment. The drawbacks were that the operation would take longer, the spleen more likely to bleed again in the post-op period, and there would be a longer convalescence until the two halves were solidly healed. Lastly, my partner and I would be at greater risk of a malpractice suit if the patient required reoperation for continued bleeding.

We discussed it. My partner was for repairing the spleen, I was inclined to remove it. Finally, I compromised—we would try a repair. If it seemed dry, we would put in a drain to monitor for re-bleeding, and close. And if the spleen did bleed again, we would promptly reoperate to remove it. He agreed. We would need to watch the patient more carefully during the next few hours, and that would be stressful. But sometimes the tough choice is the right one.

He did not re-bleed—his post-op course was smooth as silk. But the case still bothered me. Jerry's teammates showed up, and camped out at his bedside. The nurses, used to younger pediatric patients, put up with the adolescent energy. And I was glad for the lift his buddies gave my patient. Coach also came to visit. But conversation with him tightened my stomach. According to what he saw, the contact was no accident at all, but an obvious attempt to take Jerry "out of the game." I spoke to Jerry's mother. She too was outraged, the other parents equally disturbed. I waited, over the next few days, for a response from the opposing coach, opposing players, the league itself, hoping there was a gesture to prove their goodwill. There was none—no flowers, no visits, no calls or get-well cards. Nothing. Finally, a week after the injury, Jerry's father called the opposing coach. His response—no inquiry into the convalescence, no hopes for a speedy recovery, only "It was a legal play. I don't want to discuss it." Click.

For my part, I decided to give the league itself a chance to do the right thing. I mean, after all, they must be interested in kids, in sportsmanship, in moral values. Or what were they doing running a sports program? I obtained the name of the league vice-president and called him on the phone, and he assured me he would look into it. I asked to be kept informed, and expressed surprise at the callous attitude of the opposing coach. The V.P. stated that when he was coaching and an injury occurred, he never inquired into the status of an injured opposing player. Worried about a suit. I've never heard back from the V.P., and I think that tells the story.

I read a good piece in the *New York Times* a while back, I think in the Sunday magazine section. I'm sorry I can't remember the name of the author. But it was about the nature of competition. The writer was an avid tennis player, and he was celebrating his opponent, saying the opponent taught him all about his game. Not in so many words, of course, but by smacking a poor backhand or a slow serve down the line. And so on with the weak half-volley, or whatever. Without the competitor on the other side of the net, the writer would never know what was wrong with his game. He said the opponent is the best, most reliable teacher we have. And this doesn't go for just "games," but for life itself. Without someone else in the classroom, we would never raise our hand. Without the critic, no artist or writer would know where he or she is headed. Without competition, few people build a better car, or a better computer. What a poor, dangerous, evil place this world would be if every rival were considered an enemy, ultimately out to destroy us. That leaves us with two choices, to destroy the opposition or be satisfied with mediocrity.

The idea, "if you can't beat him, cripple him," has been around Washington a lot since the days of Nixon. Taken to its logical conclusion politically, it ends in chaos, the destruction of democracy. No "loyal opposition," as in Britain. And nothing gets done. On the high-school level, it glamorizes violence, with effects like Columbine. I have a good friend who coaches kids' teams in baseball and ice hockey, and he reports that the brutal competitiveness is there too. "Winning is more important than kids," is how he puts it. That's crazy! Those of us who educate children, in sports or wherever, need to understand the moral implications of what we teach. Apparently this soccer league does not. Shame on them. And shame on us if we don't do something about it.

Operating on AIDS

One day during the AIDs crisis, things were different in the operating room. You had to know what to look for to see the change. There was an altered pace and rhythm to the operation, and a tense, more sober mood: the strange headgear, the goggles and the double gloves almost signalled a denseness to the air itself. You might have thought we were operating on an unexploded bomb, and indeed we were. We were operating on a patient with AIDS.

So the operation was as risky for us as for the patient. His blood was contaminated with a poison that could kill any of us as it was destined to kill him. Scratched into the skin, or rubbed into the eye, it was a highly lethal wetness.

Then be careful, you might caution. But in a workroom of blades and needles, this was easier said than done. Moving under time pressure, protected by condom-thin gloves and permeable cloth, we would be vulnerable as never before. The patient was a young man who had come down with many of the stigmata of the disease: chronic, unexplained illness, infections, and weight loss. I don't know how he'd gotten AIDS—it didn't really matter. What did matter was that he needed an operation, and I was the one to do it.

I suppose any of us could have backed out. Or we could have sent him to a different hospital, insisting they had more experience with this sort of thing. The Hippocratic Oath does not require the doctor to risk his life. Yet from the time of St. Luke, doctors and nurses have put their lives on the line to save others. On the battlefield or in the plague-infested village, doctors and nurses have been "professionals," dedicated to a higher calling.

This day, we weren't in a remote jungle or malarial rice paddy, not some infectious disease ward. We were in our bright new hospital, in the safe, quiet town, wearing the same gray slacks and white coats, greeting the same colleagues as the day before. And then we put on our heroism and humanity with double gloves, hoods, and extra alertness.

It would have been somewhat comforting if the patient's body warned us by ticking like a time-bomb. It might have kept us more alert to the danger. For the opening of the living, breathing, human body is a vivid, rapturous act. When you're deeply into it, you can think of nothing else: unbalanced checkbooks, next week's vacation, even family problems fade before the fascination of the opened belly. What to compare it to, this messy, disorganized arrangement of guts and organs which takes in our culinary pleasures and magically transforms them into flesh, bone, energy, and excretions? There are so many miracles visible in the human abdomen that, if you're thinking at all, if you're not caught up in the plan and rhythm of surgery's ballet, your thought must be accompanied by awe.

So, distracted by the various organs before us, we could forget the danger, become careless and join the patient in his illness. There is usually a closeness in the O.R.—you lay aside petty animosities in favor of mutual dedication to the healing of another person. Those with the guts and training to enter an operating room are, for the most part, strong willed and individualistic. But we become a team when we scrub our hands together, and, almost ritualistically, give and take instruments and advice from each other. Yet on that day, beside having a common interest in our patient, we felt great protectiveness of each other. We'd signed, as it were, a pact in the patient's blood. Perhaps the camaraderie is similar to what happens on a battlefield.

During any surgery, the surgeon proceeds under two somewhat contradictory imperatives—speed and carefulness. The requirement for speed dates from the era before anesthesia and blood transfusions, when the screaming patient, leather strap in teeth, was held down by strong-arms for the life-saving amputation. A surgeon's skill was measured solely by his speed.

Even nowdays, speed is important. Anesthesia is a poison to the nervous system, disrupting connections between brain and muscle. When the patient wakes, the blood washes out these poisons, but the process adds another burden to the already taxed circulatory system. Better anesthetics have not fully relieved the surgeon's need to be quick.

Then, there is the ever-present question of money. The patient's time in the O.R. is measured both by the anesthesiologist and scrub nurse. Minutes spent in this stark, sterile, unfriendly-looking place must be the most expensive room-for-rent there is.

Lastly, the surgeon's ego. I admit to asking the nurse how long a case took, and smirking behind my mask when she said I was faster than a colleague.

Good surgery is a lot like ballet, with several scenes at different tempi. The opening and closure are done at presto, intermediate scenes adagio, the crucial part at largo. Debakey from Houston would do only the largo of his cardiac procedures, his assistants opening and closing. Thus, he could save several lives in a working day.

On the day of the AIDS patient, our tempi were unusual. All done largo, slowly, as if walking a straight line for a traffic cop. With extra headgear, drapes, and tension, we had increased attentiveness to the sharps in our hands. We observed each other moving as if underwater. I felt breathless, constricted, threatened, in a foreign place, like my first scuba dive.

We opened through a midline incision, slowly cutting layer by layer, watching the points. The organs lay in their assigned places, the mass where we expected. The patient's wasted thinness made dissection easy; his youth benefitted us all.

The deep dissection was at a slow but usual rate; we'd forgotten the risks in the fascination of the process. We divided the blood vessels between clamps, tied off, and severed the membranous films supporting the tumor. A nice dissection, my ego said. Good enough for a video for the next surgical conference. A last snip, and the tumor lay in my hands, then the stainless basin on the table.

The patient had survived. But there was still danger in the form of the patient's bloody open wound, soiled drapes, and sharp instruments.

The closing stayed adagio. The needle was passed with the same care as the scalpel. I placed a stitch, cut off the needle, then tied. No dangling needle. The last stitch in, we finally relaxed. Placed the bandages on like a benediction, hiding the danger below.

We felt good. The patient was safe, for now. Increasingly, we also, were safe, as we bagged the contaminated material and peeled off gowns and gloves. The anesthetist woke him quickly, removing piece by piece her soiled equipment. Finally, as we rolled him onto his litter, he looked up with groggy eyes into my face. I greeted him by removing my mask.

Strange, you might think, that we risked our lives in a hopeless situation. Yet we are all, ultimately, doomed to die. And the time between now and then is precious, is it not?

Megan and the Orphaned Fleas

That summer at the Cape, I'm sure our neighbors thought we had gone to the dogs. Thirteen of them, to be exact. Three of mine, two of my brother's, and eight of my sister's—a mother and litter of seven. But when the summer ended, we left the house alone, without animals of any kind, if you didn't count the mice.

Problem was, I decided to come back about two weeks later, a little weekend treat for my thirteen-year-old daughter Megan and her friend Kim. We arrived, unloaded the car and moved in. Almost—for as soon as the girls entered the front hall, they started screaming and jumping around like two banshees. Next thing, they were on the coffee table, slapping at their shins. Looking carefully in the fading light, I could see a cloud of fleas hovering about a foot off the ground. What to do?

My luck held. I had noticed, as we pulled up to the house, a mid-sized dog wandering around outside. He seemed friendly, so I stepped out the screen door and invited him over for a visit. I took him first up to bachelor's hall, on the third floor, then led him through all the bedrooms on the second floor, then dining, living, and sun porch, a full tour of the house. Finally, I escorted him out the front door.

He left, scratching. And the flea problem had ended.

Comment:

A good friend objected to this, feeling that it was unkind to the neighborhood dog. But what about the fleas? They too, I'm sure, had feelings. They had been abandoned after weeks of flea-paradise, with various-sized dogs from all over the East coast. Must have been starving. With the new development, they had a future of unlimited hides to land on rather than dry rugs until death. As for the dog's feelings, I can't answer. But he seemed accustomed to it. As for me, scratching is one of life's greatest pleasures. There are many areas I particularly relish, the middle of my back, where a good friend gives pleasure, or my tummy in the morning, or other areas I will not mention. So as regards feelings, and interactions between various species, you have to take everything into consideration.

25 Years in Brief

After graduation, I continued on the long, arduous road toward a career in surgery. I finished my residency training in 1967, then served two years in Japan, caring for the wounded from Vietnam. Following that, I returned to the states, moved to Flemington, New Jersey, and began a highly successful practice, which lasted until two years ago.

Now, as to what happened on a deeper level. The first remarkable thing was my marriage in 1961 to Erica Hamilton, daughter of Dean Hamilton of the Graduate School. She has provided the yeasty ingredients which have made life exciting and rewarding. She has also provided two daughters, with whom we are both very pleased.

But our time in Japan was a turning point for me. It reoriented my life from a narrow, Western viewpoint to a more universal one. The strangeness of the land and its people as well as the anguish of the Vietnam conflict left me a far different person than I had been before.

After Japan, I gave surgical practice eleven years, and found it rewarding financially and professionally, but unexpectedly unsatisfying on a deeper, more personal level. So much of surgery involved patching up people without making any lasting difference in their lives. And so much of it was uncreative from a personal point of view, carrying out the procedures and techniques developed by others. I felt there was little in my practice that was uniquely my own creation.

So two years ago I essentially gave up active practice, and since then have spent only 8 to 10 hours a week at the hospital. The great majority of my time has recently been spent writing about the glimpses that medical practice gives a doctor into the "human condition." Perhaps, by describing the ways by which people become sick and how they become well, I may help others benefit from my training in an unorthodox but very important way. At this point of the fascinating journey we call life, that is my intention.

Changing Partners

A divorce is hard to write about, harder still to experience. Mine still occupies a place in my soul I'd rather not enter. But, to complete my story, I must.

My first wife, Erica, was a fine person, a lovely, talented, kind-hearted lady. A partner better than I deserved. She took on the responsibilities and roles of wife and mother without complaint or error, even as I focused most of my time and attention on a busy practice. We came from similar backgrounds, had similar values, had compatible views on politics and relationships. What more could one ask for?

We never argued. That was the first clue to the rift. We never felt a disagreement large enough to quarrel about, so we never learned anything new from each other. And she was focused on art, the world of graphic representation of reality; while I increasingly pursued the word and the spiritual dimension which that represented. Each of us became increasingly skillful at our diverging interests. It doesn't seem enough to break up a union, but encouraged by friends with powerful and attractive personalities, pulling in opposite directions, it was enough.

I take full responsibility for resisting an accommodation. In my fantasy, I wanted a "soulmate," not realizing it was probably asking too much. And, given my restless tendencies, I wanted activity of a different kind than my profession had provided. Was new adventure a part of it? Perhaps so, but that may have been true for both of us after thirty years.

I bless our daughters for riding out the ensuing storm with grace and forbearance. They both made an effort to understand, to the extent that they could, and forgive two restless parents. Bless them again.

Oprah and Me

I am a restless type, always a little bored and looking for something interesting to do out of the ordinary, verging on my family's disapproval. This time I decided to write a book! As my Italian friend Giorgio is fond of saying, "Why not?" But this was even before he'd become my best friend.

What I'd noticed was that my patients didn't like surgeons. Not me anymore than any other surgeon—just in general. I didn't much care to be disliked simply because of what I did every day and how I made my living. But actually, I kind of understood. Surgeons were often nasty people. I didn't care for many of them myself. And the worst were usually the ones higher on the totem pole (cardiac surgeons, neurosurgeons, and worst of all, plastic surgeons.) One cardiac surgeon at Penn told me, after a two-month externship with him, that, knowing my father, he'd expected great things of me. But he had been disappointed! This perfect southern gentleman also made it a practice to point out to his colleague and partner how few of the partner's patients survived surgery. Of course, he always chose for himself the patients with the best prognoses. He once asked his partner where he would hold a meeting of his post-op cases, "In a phone booth?" His partner later killed himself.

But I tried to be caring, compassionate, friendly. I made it a point to treat patients with respect, take their hand when we met. My father called it "the laying on of hands." I'd ask how they felt, I'd say, "How's the wife?" "How many kids?" "Everything's going to be fine." And then, two days later in the operating room, I would take a knife, cut deeply through skin and muscle to the mysterious coiled organs beneath, and do whatever it took—coldly, with a mask on, no thought to the fact that this was a human being under me. I was without nerves, did what had to be done, no shaking hand. Then, two days later, at the patient's bedside, I would take his hand, give it a caress or squeeze, smile and tell him, or her, that he would be well. This was an emotional somersault, from a flower-arranger to a butcher. Some surgeons could do it all the time, some only part of the time. Some, never. But the coldest of them were sometimes the most skilled in the O.R. Like the perfect southern gentleman.

I thought this story needed telling so that patients could understand their surgeons' seemingly schizophrenic behavior. So I decided to write a book about why surgeons are the way they are.

My wife was not enthusiastic about the idea, but she was used to giving me space. I took a realistic look at my writing skills and decided they were less than optimal. I'd written a thesis and junior papers in college and gotten "gentlemen's Cs," but this writing would be "for real." So I took some writing courses at The New School in New York and attended writing groups in Princeton. The process took altogether eight years, as long as it had taken to learn how to operate on a human and have him survive. Then I decided, on the advice of a friend, to try to get

into the excellent Breadloaf Writer's Conference at Middlebury College. I polished a couple of chapters and was pleased to be accepted as a "manuscript student," one of those who would have his work read and critiqued in class. I should, of course, mention that all this took place under the encouragement of a far better writer than I—my wife Areta. She held a master's degree in English literature from Columbia University. And she did her generous and encouraging mentoring well—my teacher at Breadloaf, himself a Puitzer Prize-winner, ended up calling me a superb writer, which sort of meant that most dogs can be taught to walk on their hind legs.

Areta and I got to work in earnest. We chose twelve stories which illustrated various aspects of a surgical practice. We would choose the worst-written piece and turn it into the best. Then we'd choose the worst of what was left and make it the best. And so on, around the circle. We polished, one after another, fourteen times around. When we were finally happy with it, the questions came up of whether and how to get it published.

At this moment, I decided to attend my twenty-fifth college reunion. I had the required beers, slapped old buddies on their beefier backs, and heard who'd been caught cheating on his wife and was now on number two, or three. Then I spotted a classmate I'd not seen in some time. Jacques DeSpoelberch had been class president our first year and one of my four assorted roommates. And he spotted me too.

"Hi, Jacques, how are you?" And what are you doing now?

"I'm fine, Dick. I'm a literary agent. How about yourself"

"I just wrote a book."

"Let me take a look at it."

Or words to that effect. In short, Jacques sold my book to Contemporary Books, and it was published soon thereafter. How lucky can you get?

The next thing, I was sitting at home one night after dinner when the phone rang.

"Is this Doctor Weeder?"

"Yes. Who is speaking?"

" I am the producer on the "Oprah Winfrey" show. We would like you to appear on the show with your book, *Surgeon: The View from Behind the Mask*."

"And when is this?"

"Day after tomorrow."

"But I have operations scheduled that morning."

From behind me, I heard Areta jumping up and down. "Yes, Yes, Yes, Yes."

"And what is the title of the show?"

"Doctors who have written books. You will be on with four others."

"Well, I guess I could rearrange my schedule. I have nothing major that morning. What do I do?"

"Come to the Eastern Airlines counter at Newark at five tomorrow. There will be a ticket for you there. Our car will meet your flight in Chicago, and we will take care of everything from there on. The show is Wednesday morning."

And so it happened. The hotel was a Japanese one—top of the line. After a sushi breakfast, the limo picked me up and delivered me to the theater. I wandered in and found the green room. One of the other physician-authors had been in the class ahead at Princeton, and we greeted each other.

Oprah entered and, after shaking hands, made small talk. She had a surprisingly rough grasp. The producer was also there. I approached her.

"Tell me again, what is the title of the show? Doctors who have written books?"

"Well, no. we have changed the topic to, 'Doctors who admit their mistakes.' It will increase our audience."

Bait and switch. The five of us had been had.

Surgeon General

Knowing C. Everett Koop was a high point of my surgical training. I became an "extern" on his service while in medical school, assisting him at surgery and observing him in the office. He was a truly gifted surgeon. In the operating room, his technique was ballet—the best "hands" I ever saw. Not moving as fast as some, they never made a false move. He routinely performed a pediatric hernia repair "from skin to skin" in ten minutes. Best known for a widely celebrated separation of Siamese twins, he would take on any challenge with confidence and skill.

He and Dad, both heads above the crowd, competed. I only heard about it years later when my brother-in-law described a frequent dispute between Koop and my father at meetings of the Philadelphia Academy of Surgery. The question was, who was better qualified to repair hernias in children: a pediatric surgeon (meaning Koop), or a general surgeon (code for my father.) They were well matched, a collision of skills and oversized egos. But neither one let their differences affect their relationship to me.

Koop epitomized both integrity and courage. He would need both when it came to dealing with President Reagan. It is a guess, but I suspect he was recommended to Reagan by his colleague at Penn, Dick Davis, Nancy Reagan's brother. In any case, as surgeon general in the Reagan administration, Koop elevated the role from beaurocracy to leadership. Convinced of the strong connection between smoking and lung cancer, Koop attacked the tobacco industry. It was an epic battle; the industry using lies, false statistics and political influence to deny the evidence that, not only lung cancer but also heart disease, emphysema, and addiction were consequences of tobacco use. The controversy, begun before Koop's appointment in 1982, raged until 1989. Koop was adamant. Given the politics, Reagan's alternatives were to back him or fire him. Koop prevailed, and cigarette packages were then printed with the warning that the surgeon general had determined that cigarette smoking was associated with lung cancer. Remarkably, twenty years later, smoking was banned from public places, laws were passed regarding their purchase, and there followed a dramatic decrease in their use. Koop showed what one man with truth and persistence can do to effect real change.

But smoking was not the only issue for Koop. He was just as vigorous in his fight against abortion. He felt that each potential life had the right to survive. His only exception was in the case where continued pregnancy threatened the life of the mother. His arguments were always thoughtful, reasonable, and non-confrontational. Yet he had devoted himself to saving the lives of flawed children, so who can blame him for this position?

A third area where he played a major role was in the fight against AIDS. The attitude of the public was generally hostile to both gays and intravenous drug users, with little sympathy for the victims. Fortunately, Reagan himself had more understanding than his staff, and without much hesitation declared his support of Koop and the Department of Health and Human

Services. Who knows what effect having a gay son played in his attitude?

Koop mentions several other organizations that supported his efforts against AIDS. These included the American Medical Association and various gay rights organizations. Koop gave frequent talks explaining AIDS, noting that infection was not likely except for those practicing unsafe sex or sharing needles. He was able to significantly allay the widespread dread of the disease, and he mobilized support for AIDS research. His was a steady hand on the wheel, and he steered a straight course.

The Bell of the King's Ball

Seated in her living room, her Frederick Law Olmstead garden outside, Mrs. Wing described her extraordinary journey. She had asked my brother-in-law Zach, her neighbor, to introduce us after she had read *Surgeon: The View from Behind the Mask.* As she had been a nurse, the request was apt.

Her nursing career had started at the Jocelyn Clinic in Boston. She had been hired away to nurse a single patient, William Bell, the President of American Cyanamid company. Bell had been made president by its owner, James B. Duke, branching out into chemistry from his massive holdings in tobacco. And Bell's fragile diabetes deserved the tender loving care of a private, full-time nurse.

Mrs. Wing continued. One day, William Bell decided to go sailing. Not used to doing things by half, he bought a sixty-five foot sailboat with the promise of speed. So, naturally, the boat had to be entered into the Trans-Atlantic race to Spain. Bell and nurse were part of the crew.

In due course, pun intended, the boat reached Santander. They were met at the harbor entrance by a dignified launch, complete with a white uniformed captain at the bow. The captain called out, "Who are you?"

"We are Americans, racing trans-Atlantic" came the reply. And they added, in turn, "Who are you?"

"Congratulations, you are first in. And I'm the King of Spain. I'd like to invite you to a ball at the palace tonight."

And so the future Mrs. Bell danced that night with the King of Spain.

Misfire

Not all my literary efforts were successful. Areta and I embarked on a project to write a book to prepare patients for surgery. It was to be called, *A Patient's Guide to Surgery*, and it would describe the steps a patient should take before a specific operation. What areas to be shaved, what diet followed, what emotional preparation was needed before any one of twenty of the most common procedures. Macmillan Press had liked the idea, had come across with a few-thousand-dollar advance, and assigned us a young publisher. We had a few cordial meetings together. Areta and I got to work, interviewed a bunch of patients and, before long, a manuscript was in the mail. We were pleased with our work, and thought it would help a lot of patients. It had been fun being creative together—the fit was good. And we felt comfortable with the young but competent publisher.

Some time before this, I had heard a lecture in Princeton by Julian Moynihan, a local author. He had described a situation he called "editorial suttee." Suttee referred to the Indian practice whereby, on the death of a distinguished male and the lighting of his funeral pyre, the deceased wife, in her overwhelming grief, would throw herself into the flames. Sounds gruesome. But, well, funerals are sometimes strange things in different cultures.

To each his own. In any case, Moynihan had chosen the image to describe what happened to an author when his editor abandons a manuscript to, as it were, let it go up in flames.

Then, one fine day after the submission, my lovely young publisher phoned to invite me into the city for a meeting. Not in her office, we would meet at Von's, a tony restaurant in midtown. I smelled a rat.

I walked in, we found a table, and I sat down to the appetizer, one of my favorites, peanut satay. After the niceties had been shared, my editorial friend announced the reason for our meeting. She was being promoted to a higher position and would pass our manuscript on to a younger, less experienced colleague. To the strains of Gymnopedi on the sound system, I realized I had suffered editorial suttee between the peanut satay and the Eric Sati.

But, damn it all, I kept the advance. It was almost enough for a good used car.

A Quaker, for All That

My parents named me after an ancestor. That was their habit. It wasn't very imaginative. Pretty lazy, I'd say. They'd named the girls after the previous mothers, 'Carolines' going back several generations. One middle name went back to William the Conqueror. Two others went back only to grandfather Nixon. After Watergate, no relation—we were sure. I escaped being Richard Nixon Weeder. But I was Richard Stockton Weeder, after the Quaker signer of the Declaration. The family had long since stopped being Quakers. We were Presbyterians, even though most of us didn't know what that meant or how to spell it. Oh, and a few of them, the ones with money, Episcopalians. We weren't ancestor worshippers. It's just that, going back enough years, they could find names of predecessors who hadn't spent time in prison.

Being a Quaker is not very fashionable. The original title for our sect is, "Society of Friends of the Truth." But nowadays the truth is in short supply. So we usually just call ourselves "Friends," and we go to Friends meetings rather than churches, cathedrals, or synagogues.

I'd gone to a Quaker school for twelve years, but it hadn't taken. I was too much into singing, particularly hymns in church, like "A Mighty Fortress is our God." And the Quakers were, well, strange, weird. Even the nice ones. No longer wore the grey clothes and broad black hats, no longer said "thee" and "thou" And what was all that about, anyway? But you could usually spot them. So gentle, so smiling, so sweet, so unreal…until they were on the other team. Boy, could they turn mean then!

But fifty-man wards of knee-length legs, foul-smelling infections, vacant, drooling mouths, and black body bags soon changed my ideas. I became sad, and angry. Our presidents were large-scale criminals, starting phony wars to elevate their status to commander-in-chief and make them more safely re-electable.

And the questions asked me by the North Koreans lingered. Why, indeed, were we in Vietnam? What responsibility did I share for the production of the mayhem? I hadn't pulled any triggers, but I had paid for the bullets. The situation was sickening, and I was horrified in my own passive guilt. So as soon as I was back home, I found myself a pacifist, and a Quaker.

For a few years, It didn't make much difference. I had entered practice, made a good name in the hospital, watched as two daughters grew and thrived. We moved to Princeton for the better schools, I went on the board of Cricket's school. I even took a sabbatical to teach psychology and religion at the nearby George School. I studied what it meant to be a Quaker.

The concept was, though seemingly weird, basically mainstream theology. Went all the way back to Genesis. "Man is made in the image of God"—the "Imago Dei," restated by St. Thomas Aquinas. Very Catholic, very basic. But from this sprang the whole Quaker mystique. If a person had "a spark of God" in him, only the tiniest particle, he (or she) had value which should not be destroyed. To kill another was, indeed, the height of evil. If a "spark" existed in the neighbor, then change, rehabilitation, reconciliation, all were possible. The person you quarrel with today may become your valued colleague tomorrow. It happens.

I'd always thought education might be our road to eternal life, revealing what remains after one takes the last breath. I bought into Einstein's thesis that there is neither creation nor destruction of matter and energy. If my body held energy while I lived, the energy had to be somewhere after I went to sleep forever. The greatest scientist of our age believed in a sort of eternal life. How marvelous! I agreed instinctively, with every fiber of my being. But, I digress. So how, luckily, did I become an educator?

I came into schooling through the back door. As an "Overseer" of Princeton Quaker Meeting, I was involved with the annual membership survey, each of us asking twelve meeting members and attenders three questions: "How are you doing?" "Are you getting the Newsletter?" and "Is there anything Meeting is not doing that you think it should be doing?" Three members, all teachers in a local school, answered identically—"We should have a "Friends (Quaker) school here."

I reported this back to the overseers. Discussion followed.

"Let's look into it. Let's poll the community, ask the local school heads."

So we did. We raised the question, "Should there be a Friends school in Princeton?" Eight school headmasters responded unanimously "Yes," even though such a school would be competition.

The question then went to the meeting's membership. In typical Quaker fashion, discussion was extensive, covering every aspect—financial, moral, practical, political, moral again, practical again, financial again, and then on to another deadly boring discussion next month. All arguments were heard, then reheard, then discussed again in the hall. And financial, once again. The penurious tradition of Quakers was there in all its glory. I began to believe that, indeed, the Quaker could buy from a Scotsman, sell to a Jew, and make a profit.

But no one was left out of the discussion. (I'm sure many wished they had been.) The consensus was (there is always a Quaker consensus) that it was basically a good idea. The doubters had good reasons: "too expensive" (there again), "just another elitist school in a college town of elitist schools," "a strain on the limited budget and educational energies of the town," All good, well intentioned arguments. The best counter-argument was that the school would raise the educational tone in the town to a more spiritual level. Quaker schools had a reputation for emphasizing values, morality, and good relationship while cutting back on excessive competitiveness in both the classroom and playing field. Friends schools were spiritual without proselytizing, and had been for centuries.

We went to the next step. Quaker process insists on unanimity for any major decision. In our meeting poll, about 97 percent were in favor. But a few resisted the idea of establishing the school "under the care of Meeting," (the quaint Quaker terminology.) There already existed a few classrooms on campus used for Sunday (First Day) school. And these could be available to start the school. Other organizations, such as Alcoholics Anonymous, already used them weekdays. And the school's spiritual support could come from Burlington Quarterly meeting, a parent organization to Princeton Meeting.

A 'Schools Committee" was formed around the three teachers whose idea had started it all. "Weighty Friends," those having experience in Quaker education and process, joined with younger enthusiasts, myself included. My active interest was punished by making me clerk of the committee. But the sparkplug of the place was undoubtedly the head teacher, Jane Fremon. People joked about "Dick and Jane at school," but it was ninety-five percent her wisdom, her vigor, her blood, sweat, and toil.

We leaned heavily on the wisdom of "weighty friends" and the teachers among us. We made up rules and regulations, borrowing from other Friends schools. Like a newborn chick, the place opened with some cracked shell and spilled blood.

Then, over the next few years, I watched from the sidelines with pleased astonishment as the school grew and thrived. After about five years, I had found it necessary to pay more attention to my practice and my family. So I backed off, leaving space for new vigor and new ideas. Those who followed picked up the ball and scored a series of touchdowns. A new building, costing one and a half million dollars, opened fully funded. A second, duplicate, followed. The Carnegie Foundation for Education rewarded our ten-year birthday by naming the school one of the ten best in the country. Once again, my good luck had spread, like a benign infection. And the school thrived, but with no great thanks to me.

I guess a few more words are in order to explain the queerness of Quakerism. It owes a great philosophical debt to Martin Luther and his "priesthood of all believers." And to the newly printed Bible, open to everyone who could read. Also a nod to the primitive church, where all believers spoke directly to God, no pope in between.

But the more basic, distinctive, distinguishing characteristic of our little group is devotion to the truth. "Society of Friends of the Truth," was the name our sect of seekers first adopted, centuries ago. Quakers past and present have been penalized, some with their lives, for being unable, with George Washington, to tell a lie. Expediency, the end justifies the means, has long been a guiding principal for the Catholic Church. Indulgences, the purchase of salvation, was Luther's main complaint. Nowadays, we count how many ruined altarboys it takes to pry a monsiegneur from his pulpit. What meaningless price, it seems to me, that the church pays to keep its priests celibate.

Building Character

The unexamined life is not well lived.

Dishonesty is like landing a plane
without seeing the ground.

As I became increasingly self-aware, particularly under the influence of my father, I set out the dimensions of the person I wanted to be. Honesty was first, predicting the increasing interest I would later have in Quakerism and its devotion to the truth. Honestly, seeing it as it really was, seemed central. Otherwise, you were in a fog, trying to bring your plane in for a landing with no vision of the ground.

Then I became aware that, as I treated others, I inevitably and ultimately treated myself. If I was gentle and understanding with myself, I was likewise gentle and forgiving of those around me. Or if I cursed myself, I cursed my neighbor, and thus became alone.

Next, I recognized the importance of sensitivity. When insensitive, I lost track of those around me and my relationship with them. I became aware early in my career as a singer that I couldn't reach my audience if I didn't "let it all hang out." If my feelings were hidden, I couldn't reach theirs. This was the center of the musical relationship. The hard shell, the callused tone, was anathema.

As a doctor, a surgeon, it was the same. I could have been cold, impersonal, as I cut deeply. Many surgeons could do no other, as I described in my first book. It was easier on the nervous system to be callous, hurt less if I didn't participate in the pain. But I wanted to provide the next dimension of medicine, be a healer, join in mending the wound I had found necessary to reach the patient's flaw.

And then, in my career as writer, sensitivity was the name of the game. As in singing, revealing my soul was the only way to reach the soul of the reader. To demonstrate what is in me, I've had to rip open the skin and muscle to uncover the guts down deep. Painful, but needed.

Getting back to honesty, it should not be an issue in politics, but it surely is. Resulting from its lack, we are in a miasma of misunderstanding, anger, chaos, and division. Many of our leaders have been seduced by our master seducer into the foulness of corruption. They're nothing more than mind-asleep lackeys.

Horsing Around

I've always been less than fond of horses. Sure, I had the infantile love affair with *Black Beauty* and *National Velvet* and Elizabeth Taylor, but maturity gave way to a different opinion. First change occurred when a close friend of my brother, an Olympic equestrian, died under her horse. And I always recoiled when I looked at my grandfather's formal portrait in his fox-hunting pinks, with his pig-like eyes (which I inherited) always following me around whichever dining or living room the painting occupied. He, name of Horace Nixon, (no relation—after Watergate—we were quite sure) was a master trick-rider, riding three horses at once (a foot on each of two, another in the middle). Or vaulting onto or off the horse. Another trick was to bribe one or another of us cousins to do his bidding. In other words he was more comfortable dealing with animals than people, and better at it. And he was a good friend of the naturalist writer, Thornton Burgess.

But the recurring experience I had by way of the emergency room was seeing motorcycle ("murdercycle," according to a colleague) accidents caused by the stupidity (or inebriation) of the rider, while horse accidents were caused by the misbehavior of the unsentient beast. So I took my prejudice out on my daughters by breaking family tradition by keeping them off the admittedly noble steeds.

Actually, the family tradition had been earlier broken by my dad. He had, in approved courting style, taken to riding with my mother when he could. I don't know whether this included "riding to the hounds" (or foxes) which she and Grandfather did every day before the school or work day started. But in any case, Dad's involvement ended the day he fell off his animal jumping into a pigpen, and then falling off again jumping out. But he did, thankfully for posterity, continue courting mom.

My last horse story happened at dinner at a friend's house. I mentioned that I worked at Hunterdon Medical Center, and one of the guests recounted a family experience at the hospital. Her father had made the mistake of passing behind her horse while putting the pet out to field. The horse, as is their wont, had reared up and kicked him in the stomach. He landed on a litter outside the x-ray department at Hunterdon. As he was waiting there, a doctor came by and asked why he was there. The father started to tell the tale, then began slurring his speech, then lapsed into unconsciousness. The doctor took one look, grabbed the litter, bypassed x-ray, and pushed it rapidly into the operating room. Ten minutes later, the father's fractured spleen and a large amount of his blood was in a silver pan. The guest ended her tale. I finished it by quietly stating, "I was that doctor."

My experience with skiing wasn't much more positive. Really, not my experience but that of a close colleague scrub nurse. She had gone skiing at a local slope when, suddenly under the influence of a second cup of coffee, she had to relieve herself at the top of the slope. Encumbered by long pants, and fully laced into her skis, she decided to squat by the side of the slope in a small group of low bushes. Pulling her pants down, she assumed her position and started the routine when, slowly but inexorably she started to drift downhill backwards, across the open slope. Held firmly in her squat, she slid by the downhill crowd into the trees on the opposite side and struck a tree, smashing one leg. By the time the ski-patrol reached her for her trip to the hospital, she had regained enough dignity to cover her behind.

But the worst was not, one might say, behind her. A good sport, not wanting to ruin her partner's weekend, she opted to spend the night at the lodge and appeared the next day by the fireside with a book. Lo and behold, the door opened and a good-looking stranger appeared in the door between crutches. He hobbled his way to another fire-side chair and eased into it. Noting her leg on a hassock, he nodded to her. She, friendly, opened by requesting his story. He replied that he'd been minding his own business the previous afternoon, passing down the slope, when he was almost hit from behind by a bare-assed crouching woman sliding backwards. Laughing uncontrollably, he then hit a tree, breaking his leg. "What happened to you," he asked.

"I'd rather not say."

Notes on a Surgical Practice

There are several points I'd like to make about the office practice of surgery. But I'd like to start out by saying a little bit about what it feels like to do surgery, as this informs all the rest I will begin by reading a short chapter from my book *Surgeon: The View from Behind the Mask*. This chapter describes an unusual problem, and how it was worked out. The chapter is entitled "The Slipping Rib," and what it is will become clear as we go along.

OPENNESS

This chapter illustrates several things about surgical practice. It illustrates first of all an openness to the patient's complaint, a willingness to listen, think, and research the problem until a solution becomes apparent. It shows the doctor in his role of detective—a role immortalized by Sir Arthur Conan Doyle in his Sherlock Holmes mysteries. As you may know, Conan Doyle was a doctor, and the similarity between his detective method and the way we make a clinical diagnosis was no accident. While

I was in medical school I took a summer in England absorbing this way of making a clinical diagnosis by looking, listening, and touching. It is fine to use x-rays and laboratory tests to confirm the diagnosis. But the doctor is much closer to the patient, and his instincts become much more accurate if he puts his primary trust on clinical findings rather than an x-ray or lab test.

CARING

A second thing illustrated by this passage is the question of caring. The surgeon is depicted here as caring for his patient's welfare, both physical and emotional. He wants to help her become pain-free, but in the process deals with her very gently and with understanding. In thinking about it, I've come to the conclusion that we care about patients in three distinct ways. First of all, on a very basic level, a surgeon cares about the craftsmanship of his work on a patient. That is, in the same way as a furniture-maker, he cares about how his job looks when it is finished and how well it functions. If it is a hernia to be repaired, he cares that it is solid, doesn't fall apart. If it is a breast incision, he cares that it is not disfiguring.

Second, a surgeon cares for his or her reputation. If he has to earn a living by his practice, and most of us do, he cares that patients appreciate his care enough to recommend him to other people. Otherwise, his practice soon shrinks or, worse yet, he gets sued for malpractice. This self-centered kind of caring is not a very noble motive, but, admittedly, it still results in good patient care.

Third, and this motive is the hardest to measure, the good physician cares about patients from humane, more spiritual motives—out of loving kindness, from empathy, from a feeling of human connectedness. This highest motive is sometimes hard to maintain when a doctor is tired or ovestressed. But it is the one the best surgeon tries to attain.

TEACHER

Now I'd like to talk about the surgeon in one of his or her other roles—that of teacher and advisor. A good teacher helps the patient become aware of his disease, its implications, and the various ways it may be helped. How much time a surgeon needs to devote to this teaching session depends on several factors—the complexity of the problem, the pre-existing knowledge of the patient, and the emotional pressures of the diagnosis. By this latter, I mean—to what extent is the situation one that the patient finds hard to deal with? For instance, if it is a question of cancer, the patient may be so emotionally overwhelmed by the diagnosis that all the teaching the surgeon attempts is lost in the patients' distracted inattention. The patient may be so caught up in thoughts of pain or death that he or she cannot even hear the suggestions the surgeon is making for treatment. So a surgeon may have to schedule more than one session with the patient—the first to discuss the diagnosis, a second, even a third, to go over treatment options. I routinely see patients with breast cancer three or more times before we carry out the definitive surgery. They are so dazed the first time or two, they don't even hear me, let alone be capable of a well informed decision.

Corollary to this teaching is the surgeon as salesman. A surgeon must sell his patient on an operation, particularly when the condition suffered is not painful. An operation is never fun, often painful, sometimes dangerous, and usually expensive. A surgeon must overcome all of these negatives in the patient's thoughts and make him or her more than willing to undergo surgery. Being such a salesman has made me appreciate the skills involved, and I consider salesmanship a worthy art.

CONFIDENTIALITY

Confidentiality is, of course, an important part of this process—confidentiality on the part of the surgeon, but also on the part of the staff. In order for a patient to feel comfortable and open to the questions asked by the surgeon, he or she needs to know that what is going on will not become the subject of gossip or news. The need for confidentiality varies from patient to patient—it is more important to some than others. But it is a factor that must always be considered.

CONSENTS

The operative consent is an important part of the preoperative procedure. At some point, preferably after he has fully explained the operation he plans to do, the surgeon must obtain permission from the patient, or his guardian if he's not a competent adult. This so-called "consent" must be specific, but should make allowances for any unexpected deviation from the planned procedure. This is one of the most important items of paperwork that goes into the patient's chart, as it functions as a sort of contract between the surgeon and patient. If anything goes wrong during the operation, the consent is the first document examined in a law court. And the consent, beside being specific, must fully reflect the information given by the surgeon in his role as teacher.

SECOND OPINIONS

A surgeon should always be open to a patient's obtaining another opinion regarding a course of treatment. There are exceptions to this: when there is not time or means of doing so, such as in an emergency or when there is no qualified person around to render the second opinion. Sometimes a second opinion can be skipped when the thing speaks for itself and the course of action is obvious. But with these exceptions, a surgeon who is unwilling to let the patient obtain a second opinion places his competence in question while denying the validity of the patient's feelings. The competent surgeon welcomes the opinion of another, unless the second opinion is to be rendered by a doctor unfriendly to the surgeon. In this case a third person should be called, one acceptable to all concerned.

When a second opinion is suggested, the first surgeon should make available all pertinent lab tests, x-rays, as well as his work-up and assessment of the situation to the doctor rendering the second opinion. If they both agree on treatment, fine. If they don't, a third opinion should be sought.

Be aware that there are at least two types of second opinion. First, there is the question about what is to be done. And second, there may be a question about who is to do it. This second opinion is, essentially, an opportunity for the patient and his family to find if there is a surgeon they feel more comfortable with than the first one. Both types of second opinion may be a waste of time and money. For instance, if the family doctor has referred the patient in for, say, a hernia repair, and the surgeon agrees that a repair is needed, there have already been two opinions rendered. Or, in the second instance, if the patient, the referring doctor, and the patient's family all feel very happy with the surgeon, it might be a waste of time and effort to see another surgeon.

AVAILABILITY

My father used to say that, next to ability, availability was the most important trait for a surgeon to have if he wished to be successful. It is certainly true that both referring physicians and patients want to be able to reach their surgeon when he is needed. And it is the job of the surgeon's office staff as well as his family to make sure that he can be contacted at all times. Coming from a surgeon's family, I learned this lesson very early in life. When my parents were out for the evening, I would be deputized to sleep by the phone in their bedroom, their whereabouts on a pad by my side, so that I could reach my father if needed. Many is the time I reached him at a concert or dinner party to get him to call the hospital or another doctor.

HUMOR

A sense of humor is a precious thing, particularly in a surgeon's office. But humor must be used with the same care as a knife, for it can do as much harm as good. The doctor and his staff must be very sensitive to a patient's mood and needs. If something funny can be said at the right time, so much the better. But if the patient has just had bad news, such as a diagnosis of cancer, no funny story is appropriate. The greatest social skills are needed in this situation. On the other hand, when the patient has become a good friend, a cheerful or funny tale can brighten the air and bring a therapeutic belly laugh. Be aware of humor—use it when the time is right.

Patient Travels

PATIENT TRAVELS CROSS-COUNTRY FOR SURGERY BY DR. WEEDER

Cynthia Blankenbaker had been suffering from "girdling chest pains" and felt like she couldn't take a deep breath - for years. After dozens of tests and numerous diagnoses by different doctors, the Oregon woman had just about given up on getting any relief from her pain. Then she picked up the book _Surgeon_, by **Richard Weeder, M.D.**, a general surgeon on the medical staff of Hunterdon Medical Center. She came to the chapter about "slipping rib condition" and recognized her condition right away.

"It was like he wrote that chapter about me," Mrs. Blankenbaker said from her hospital bed at HMC last week. After reading the book, she looked up Dr. Weeder and had him send her additional information about the condition. But she wasn't able to find a surgeon in her area who knew anything about the condition or the surgery required to correct it. Once again she contacted Dr. Weeder and arranged to travel to New Jersey to have the procedure performed at Hunterdon Medical Center.

Slipping rib condition is "abnormal mobility of the anterior interchondral articulations of the 8th, 9th and 10th ribs," explained Dr. Weeder. Many patients with the condition recall a past trauma to the effected area, he said. Some examples of patients he has treated include a woman who fell while skiing, an elderly woman whose son-in-law gave her too tight of a "bear hug," and a pastry chef who injured herself while lifting a 40-pound container of icing.

Dr. Weeder said he performs surgery to correct slipping rib condition once or twice a year. The surgery requires a short hospital stay, and in some cases can be performed on an outpatient basis.

Mrs. Blankenbaker and her husband Ben flew out from Grant's Pass in southwestern Oregon on Monday, February 14. Dr. Weeder performed the surgery the following day, and the Blankenbakers returned home on Wednesday, February 16.

After years of doctor visits, tests and medical bills, the three-day trip was well worth it, said Mrs. Blankenbaker just hours after her surgery. "Everyone here has been absolutely wonderful, and everyone knows about slipping ribs here," she said. She quipped about her ordeal, "I guess your ribs can't slip on the west coast; you have to come to the east coast for that to happen."

Going East

I ran into a physician not long ago who had served in Nixon's white house. This is his story.

Before Kissinger and Nixon visited China, this doc had travelled there in advance to "scope out" Chinese medicine in case anyone in the contingent became ill. After reporting back, he then returned to China with Nixon, Kissinger, and "Scotty" Reston, Nixon's press secretary, (formerly of the *New York Times*.) All went according to plan until Scotty became ill. The diagnosis was acute appendicitis. What to do next?

My informant was consulted—there was no Western-trained surgeon in their group, so the Americans would have to use a Chinese surgeon for the appendectomy. And this surgeon recommended acupuncture as the anesthesia of choice. Scotty asked my informant his advice about this, and he, having seen acupuncture during his information-gathering, thought it a good choice. So Scotty underwent surgery under acupuncture alone, without Western drugs or inhalant gases. As promised, Scotty had no significant pain during the procedure, and his recovery was smooth. Another benefit: the Press Secretary had none of the side-effects of Western sedatives and narcotics.

On his return, Scotty reported his experience in the Times. And that news article, more than anything else, led to the widespread adoption of acupuncture in the West. Furthermore, many Western physicians opened their minds to other aspects of Oriental medicine, discovering the benefits of its many modalities, drugs, and ancient, alternate wisdom. The Chinese had a medical history as old as ours, but approached health and healing from a very different point of view than that of Hippocrates, Paracelsus and Osier. While Nixon opened the West to Chinese culture and government, Scotty Reston introduced one of the marvels of Eastern medicine.

I can't attest to an extensive knowledge of acupuncture, but this is how my wife and I have used it. First of all, as a general "toner" that one might gain from a massage or gentle exercise. It's hard to know what measurable effects this has, but in terms of sleeping well, fewer aches and pains, and general good feeling, there is no question of its benefits. When we have described our specific areas of discomfort, our acupuncturists have usually been able to provide relief.

But we have also witnessed more dramatic findings. A couple come to mind. Two of the unpleasant side effects of radiotherapy given to treat head and neck cancer are the loss of sense of taste and a dry mouth. I met a patient who had suffered both problems for over two years. Then he had an acupuncture treatment which relieved his complaints within a couple of hours. And his disabilities were cured permanently.

Even more persuasive was the information I got from a professor of anesthesia at Penn. The occasion was a conference on head and neck cancer. The subject of post-radiation dry mouth came up, and acupuncture treatment mentioned. During the discussion, I asked the professor how many patients had their dry mouth/loss of taste reversed by acupuncture. His answer was sixty percent—a high enough number for any skeptic!

Even more persuasive was our experience with dry eye. We have seen persons suffering from dry eye to "tear up" within minutes of an acupuncture treatment. This remedy may need repeating from time to time, whereas the reversing of dry mouth seems permanent.

For a Westerner used to having straightforward mechanical or chemical explanations of medical phenomena, I find this amazing. When I quiz acupuncturists, they say that acupuncture is transmitted through "meridians" that are unrelated to the nervous system. O.K., but I still don't understand it! I guess I need to tell myself, with Hamlet, "There are more things in heaven and earth, Horatio, than are dreamt of in your philosophy." There are gifts of knowledge and practice in Eastern medicine that still remain obscure to our Western minds. We need much more study of Eastern practice to complete the picture of how healing occurs.

Working Together for Patients

It is always interesting when former "enemies" are obliged to work together for a common goal, whether in sports or international politics. Such a scene is now being played out in medical care to an increasing degree, with a growing movement toward the inclusion of historically adversarial treatment modalities into the same therapeutic plan. We are using surgery and antibiotic care now in conjunction with homeopathy, biofeedback, herbalism, and acupuncture, to name a few of these "alternative" modalities. Instead of being alternative, they are becoming complementary. And the patient is the winner in this new development!

Andrew Weil, M.D., is perhaps the best-known example of the trend for "Western" doctors to inform themselves of the other camp. His book *Spontaneous Healing* is a balanced explanation of how various health systems may interact and complement each other. I recommend it. Very useful for the cancer patient is *Getting Well Again* by O. Carl Simonton, M.D. et al. It presents practical information on how the immune system may be mobilized through innovative and non-traditional ways to fight cancer.

We in the Western, "scientific," tradition have always had the easier time proving our remedies—we have usually concentrated on short-term illnesses where cure could be measured by an improving x-ray, a pathological report, a blood chemistry, or a dropping fever. Meanwhile, the herbalists, acupuncturists, and chiropractors have been struggling with chronic complaints where progress was difficult or impossible to measure. Those of us with M.D. after our name should have understanding and sympathy with our brothers and sisters in the other healing arts. For our patients' sakes, it is time for open minds all around.

Evidence is gathering in the scientific literature to support this trend. Double-blind, reproducible studies are supporting the efficacy of many alternative remedies. The discipline "psychoneuroimmunology" has traced the connections between emotions, hormone production, and cellular immunity which many of us have suspected all along but were unable to prove and therefore act upon. A careful British study on homeopathy has come to the conclusion that it either works or the scientific method is itself flawed!

I am delighted to report that many of us at Hunterdon Medical Center are actively investigating alternative health care modalities. A committee has been organized to prioritize these systems for review. Programs have been and are being scheduled so that we may educate ourselves. We are beginning to incorporate some of these complementary disciplines into the hospital setting, and will be doing more of this. And we are changing our individual practices to be sensitive to an expanding array of useful therapies.

Repairman and Copyist

I've spent my life traveling between two careers, those of repairman and copyist. The things I've been repairing are bodies, in my training as a surgeon. And, as a writer, I've been copying on paper thoughts of skies, and happenings, and feelings. These two strokes are opposite but complementary, a sort of yin and yang of career. And I need to contemplate them.

I gave up the repairing a few months ago. It was difficult work, rather tricky, as you couldn't stop the watch—had to keep it going while you rearranged the parts, or it would never tick again. And if, somehow, things didn't work out, they could take away the repair shop and living quarters to punish me for my clumsiness. I had the constant feeling of walking uphill on a knife-edge.

So, I'm glad it's over, the repair work. I'd never felt myself the best repairman that ever lived, though that's what patients wished me to be (rather see me perfect than human). Opposite from the way they want their God—something they can see, touch, and who can forgive them one-on-one, complete with guarantees. Some docs do think themselves God—but they always get their comeuppance.

Copyists too put on godly airs, calling themselves "creative," "artistes," self-indulgent with berets, temper tantrums, and affairs. Yet none of us can make a flower. We may copy it with paint or marble, evoke it with rhyme, music, or dance. But not, honest to God, make it. A dog does not understand calculus. What makes us think we can imagine, let alone carry out, creation?

So, I'll go on copying, hoping I'll remind someone of something good. The good is always worth copying, or so they tell me. And the most important things in life are what we leave behind.

I gave up the repair work once before, in mid-career, to write about the craft of surgery. I wanted to let patients know what makes surgeons tick. I gave it up for ten years—that's how long it took me to learn to express myself in a new way. Just about as long as it took me to learn to do surgery! I took courses close to home and at the New School in NYC. Also a stint at Bread Loaf in Vermont. I did it seriously. In my mind, it was not goofing off or second-rate work. Who knows who my writing might affect? So I had to do it right.

I published a book, and it went through a second edition in paperback. A few radio interviews, and a spot on the Oprah Winfrey show did a lot for my ego, but not for my bank account. Reality hit one day at tax time. My accountant said that I had to earn some money or go broke. And the writing wasn't going to do it. I decided to pick up the scalpel again. So, with a bit of good timing and support from my partners, I returned to my surgical practice.

It wasn't as if I had been completely away from surgery. During the time writing, I had kept my hand in by assisting my partners with their most difficult cases. I'd kept up my credentials and licenses with continued medical education courses. I was aware of the newest advances in my specialty.

This was in the early nineties and laparoscopic surgery was just becoming the "gold standard" for gall bladder conditions. I took a course and started doing the procedure at same time my colleagues at the hospital took it up. We assisted each other, especially at first, and I found the procedure to be a fun challenge. It is, technically, rather a weird business like mending socks while looking in a mirror, and using tools backwards and upside down. I felt like the newest resident in training once again. We envied the kids who could do computer games with "joysticks." The trick now was to go very slowly, never going beyond what you could really see, and then "opening" the patient if you felt the least bit out of control. Gall bladder surgery had long been my favorite operation, and the laparoscopic technique quickly assumed the same place. The O. R. nurses and anesthesiologists were kind enough (they could follow my every move on the monitor) to tell me I did a terrific "lap chole." For a time, we made a video of every case, reviewing the early ones to check our technique. But before long we had boxes of these, and then filmed only the cases which might prove unusual or complicated.

Doing the other cases, like colon resections, mastectomies and the like was no problem as I had been assisting my colleagues on a regular basis. The only questionable case was the hernia repair. I hadn't seen one in ten years, as my partners never asked for my help with these relatively minor procedures. Yet, for the fact that it is both common and safer than most other operations, the hernia repair is a complex procedure from an anatomical point of view. The steps involved in the routine Bassini or Shouldice repairs, the ones most common at the time, were multiple, and involve an encyclopedic knowledge of the region. I wasn't sure how it would go. For the first hernia, on a child, there was no problem. With C. Everett Koop at Penn, I helped with many of these. He was the most superb surgeon I'd ever known. So this day, I just mimicked him, step by step. The next hernia was a routine adult, the third a complicated repair. Certainly, I knew what I would do, but it didn't seem it would be as easy as the kiddy had been.

I made the incision. Then, to my astonishment, my hands took over and proceeded, one motion after another. My hands had recalled just what to do! It was like playing on the piano a long memorized Brahms waltz without the score before me. My hands re-taught my mind the hernia repair, step by step. And when it came time for the complicated hernia, the third one, my mind was back in control, going through it in full awareness.

We think that our tissues are all "specialists," our muscles knowing how to contract, our tendons to hold fast, our bone to support, our nerves to carry thoughts. But they all arose from one paired cell, product of two parents, which then divided and differentiated into the variety we call organs. Yet those cells remember back to when they were plenipotent, able to become any kind of cell. And they remember other things. I have two places in my body that remember traumas—a chronically pulled groin muscle that remembers the taunts of my soccer coach, when each kick caused pain. Or the spot on the sole of my foot where my surgeon-father painfully dug out bits of a rubber sneaker impaled by a nail. How I hated my father at that moment. There must be other parts of my anatomy that remember things which my mind has long forgotten—a first coitus, a slap on the face, a blow to the belly. Who knows? I recently heard a lecture which described tales from an organ transplant team;

a heart recipient started using a word not in his, but his donor's, vocabulary. Or another young heart recipient described the man who had killed her donor, seeing him in a recurrent nightmare. What a wondrous thing this body is, able to do so many things, and remember things beyond remembering. As we listen to the music of Mozart or Bach, does the rhythm come from only the head, or perhaps also from the heart-pulse, or even the gut? I think, at least from all these three. And, perhaps, from something beyond.

Lucky Cousin

It is hard to deny that my efforts to do unusual and unconventional things have been stimulated by rumors, true or false, of stars in my family history. The first, of course, was Richard Stockton, after who I was named. A signer of the Declaration, once a Quaker, he was one of four who brought (bribed) the University from Elizabeth, New Jersey, to Princeton while it was still the "College of New Jersey." He recruited John Witherspoon to be President of the college, another signer, and his law clerk was James Madison, who wrote The Bill of Rights for our young democracy. Even today, I pass by his gravestone at Princeton Meeting with reverence. But I also curse him as I cross campus from side to side on a hot summer day, for giving the university so much land. Yet he was not my direct ancestor. My direct descent is from his grandfather, the first Richard Stockton, who bought six thousand acres from another cousin, William Penn. My direct ancestor in this line was William Crispin, who surveyed Philadelphia for Penn and was Pennsylvania's first chief justice. An honorable but relatively poor cousin.

Way back was "Richard the Fearless," Duke of Normandy in 963, and the father of William the Conqueror, known as "William the bastard." What does the illegitimate son of a duke have to do to justify himself to his parent but conquer a country and make himself a king? Originally from Italy, the family name had been "Crispinis" and they had been Grimaldis. Thus the Crispins remained cousins of the king.

Only family lore supports all this. The story that a Nixon, grandfather's ancestor, had proclaimed to the public, in Philadephia, the newly signed Declaration of Independence. Or that Richard Nixon was a relative, which the family vigorously denied, but only after Watergate. But my brother was named "Dana Nixon Weeder." I could very easily have been "Richard Nixon Weeder." Heaven forbid.

Grandmother Weeder came from wealth. But, fortunately for me, her brothers had wasted it, so she was obliged to use her operatic voice to put Dad through med school.

And there was my uncle, whose father had partnered with J.P. Morgan in the railroad business. He came to my wedding in his railroad car.

Growing up, I was faced with the story of my father's Penn anatomy students having dubbed him "The prince of Wales" for his charisma. He'd been the first in the city to remove a cancerous lung, served as professor of surgery in three of the city's med schools. How could I fulfill his kindly prediction that I would be the better surgeon? I had to figure out how cancer works and write a book about it.

But I remain the poor cousin, unspoiled by dollars in the pocket. How lucky can you get?

Lucky Guess

BEING AWARE

My favorite story from all the sacred literature involves The Buddha. A wise man from a noble Indian family, he apparently evolved into a gigantically holy being, an example of the end-stage spiritual maturation described by Piaget and Kohlberg and illustrated in Malcolm X's autobiography. But the story goes something like this.

Three wise men were traveling and came upon the Buddha, meditating under a Bo tree. One of the wise men asked, "Buddha, are you God?"

"No, I am not God,"

The next wise man asked, "Buddha, are you a prophet?"

"No, I am not a prophet."

The third, becoming impatient, then asked, "Well, if you're not God, and you're not a prophet, who are you?"

"I am aware (awake)."

Meditation seems to result in this. While seemingly lazy, meditation enjoins the "monkey mind" to slow, it permits the water to clear, the spasm to relax. It brushes away the cobwebs to allow for a clearer vision, perhaps a glimpse of the divine spark at the bottom of the soul. It reveals reality, fostering the growth of the personality toward sainthood and universal understanding. Gandhi found it, Mother Theresa also, and Martin Luther King. Robert F. Kennedy was getting close, as was Malcolm X.

But the question of the search for truth had a medical aspect. As a medical student, I had been fond of mystery novels, particularly Sherlock Holmes and Agatha Christie. I was aware that the author of the Sherlock Holmes stories was a physician, Sir Arthur Conan Doyle, and that the great detective's deductions followed the same techniques used in English medical diagnosis. Seemingly unrelated bits of information could be collated to provide a brilliant diagnosis. Often ignored were lab studies and x-rays. I'd seen that happen when, one day on the pier at Hyannisport, my father saw John F. Kennedy being transferred by stretcher to an ambulance. Dad looked at me and quietly declared, "He has Addison's disease." The young senator's malady was revealed to Dad not by the press but only by linking JFK's weakness and darkened skin color. Dad's awareness of a closely guarded secret was a revelation to me. I determined to develop that skill.

Opportunity had presented when I was contemplating the honeymoon Erica and I were to take to Europe. Starting in Rome, we planned to pick up a tiny Fiat, drive north through France, cross into England, and finish by visiting Eri's Scottish relatives. I'd heard it was possible to take a brief externship in physical diagnosis at St. Bartholomew's legendary London hospital. I'd jumped at the chance. And so I met some of the most reknown diagnostitions in the world. Reginald Scowen, a cardiologist, was one. He spoke to our small group sporting the most enormous stethoscope I'd ever seen. Popular at Penn at the time was the tiny Littman, with a quarter-sized bell and tubes short enough to risk catching the patient's cold. But Sir Reginald's instrument carried a bell big enough for a cow and thick rubber tubes reaching almost to the floor. One of us asked the professor about this. With a smile, he declared that the important distance was not between the doctor's ears and the patient's chest, but between the doctor's ears.

And so I had became the best diagnostition in whatever hospital I served. Starting my intern year, first rotation, first day as an intern, I was presented with a middle-aged black woman. Complaint, "tiredness." I asked about sleep habits, diet, exercise, all the usual. Then the unusual, "Any change in your skin color?" "Now what in hell?" you might ask. But the answer came back, "Yes, I've been getting darker recently."

I picked up the phone and called the admitting medical resident. "I've got a lady down here with Addison's disease," I said.

"You're crazy," he replied. I described the story, and he decided to humor this wet-behind-the-ears intern by admitting the patient. A few days later, the lab reports came back—abnormal adrenal gland function.

But the kicker in the story was that the patient was the housemaid for the Penn medical school Professor of Endocrinology!

Now how about cancer? What we'd been doing was to remove tumor. I got into an argument with the President of the Cancer Control Society on the West coast about what was "cancer control" and what was "cancer cure." But cancer cure, as we've been practicing it, is a bit like treating a broken leg by an amputation—takes care of the problem, but does not return function very well. True cure is to restore the affected organ to normal anatomy and function. And that aim, to my mind, is not well served by surgical removal, radiological removal, or poisoning of the organ. The only proper cure is the stimulation of the body's immune cells, the T cells, to attack and eat the rogue cancer cells. Or even better, as it turns out, is to alter the genetic abnormality that results in rogue cells.

The epiphany came to me one night in Honolulu. It was midnight, I was lying on the cot on our lanai, gazing up at Orion's belt to the refrain of the surf on Waikiki. And it suddenly came to me, the answer to the three riddles I'd challenged my oncologist friends with: The spontaneous remission of the patient with terminal cancer; the deadly recurrence, after personal tragedy, of the fifteen-year "cured" patient; or the five-pack-a-day who does not get lung cancer. It had to be the immune system which provided remission and recovery of health. And as it turns out, my lucky guess was right. And so we taught a class of cancer patients how to stimulate their T cell production. And I published, *The Key to Cancer*.

Thoughts on Healing

"The Letter Killeth, the Spirit Giveth Life"
II Corinthians, 3:6

I find it very hard to label people nowadays; those who used to be "conservative" are now putting the nation in debt while liberals are voicing fiscal restraint. And "right to life" for one means loss of freedom for another, pitting mother against offspring. And so on. We are caught up in a swamp of definitions and labels, few of which seem to be what they say.

I used to think in polar terms: Republicans were the opposite of Democrats, liberals the opposite of conservatives. Now I look at them as yin and yang, complementing each other, defining each other as dark defines light, and vice versa. And I see us, as individuals, partaking of one posture one moment, another the next. We may be conservative economically while liberal theologically. And we may move from one to the other as we mature.

Yet as I look more deeply into the question, it seems to me that people fall into one of two types: those who wrap themselves in the armor and shield of a group or an idea, following a rigidly laid-out program for life, usually claiming that those not in their group are misguided. The other camp consists of individuals on a search, moving from one discovery to another with wonder and openness. They walk a curved path of opportunity and risk, relying on instinct and faith as their guides. When they reach a fork in the road, they choose one without great certainty and hope it is best.

I suppose I am more seeker than finder. Those who have found "truth," it seems to me, are less open to inspiration or paradox, are uncomfortable with shades of gray, are more likely to separate themselves from others around them. Problem is, there may be more than one "true" answer to a puzzle.

I first became aware of this in harmony class in college. The professor gave us a melody to harmonize, and we all set to work. When we had finished, less than enchanted with the results, he played us J.S. Bach's harmonization of the tune. I was delighted! It was perfect, just right. But then the professor presented Bach's second answer to the puzzle; every bit as lovely, and a third, likewise. I was astonished. How could there be several right answers to a single question?

My father had an answer to every question. And they were usually good and intelligent. But I was wary of them because they were so often accompanied by bombast. How could he be so sure? And, if he was so sure, why did he need to drive it home with such force?

I have wandered through life a bit unsure, tentative. I smile, am pleasant, and let people push me around a little. I rarely respond with the quick quip or bon mot, and regret the lost opportunity later. But that's the way I've molded myself, or been molded.

I've been struck by how many things, even common things, we can't explain. We are all aware of gravity since our first fall as infants. Yet who really understands how or why it works? Physicists talk about mass, and so on. But then why doesn't something with greater density fall faster than something with less?

Or how to explain love? We all know it and feel it in another. But how, in the last resort, do you prove it? Enlightened self-interest? Perhaps, but more than that. Mutual attraction? That may be a part of it. Mutual dependency? Often true. But love that motivates our strongest impulses cannot be explained by these only. In human terms, love is as powerful and omnipresent as gravity, and just as mysterious.

Or consider the question of proving the existence of God. It was the topic of my college senior thesis, but I've long ago given up on that puzzle. I am left with, "I don't know." In my best moments, I have faith. But I have to be content with that and comforted that others far smarter than I admit to uncertainty.

Early in life I developed a bad habit of "not filling my head with things I didn't need," as if my brain had a limited capacity. I regret this now—my head was plenty large enough to accommodate all I encountered. And the habit of letting things slide away lost me a lot of ideas that could have come in handy; it made my memory a sieve. Shelves stocked three-deep with ideas is a precious resource.

So now, as a writer, I collect ideas, as if butterflies with a net. I try to keep the ego out of the way and open myself to whatever inspiration comes along. I examine the ideas I've gathered, a collector pinning his specimens to a board. I test them against experience and accepted principles. Then I write them down for later use.

I've rejected legalism in favor of the spirit. Not that laws aren't needed, but they undermine the creative impulse and the urge to do good works according to the more instinctive conscience. They are binding rather than freeing. As Bart Giamatti, the President of Yale, described the liberal education: it liberates one to accomplish whatever is possible.

William Penn, trained in the law, complained that, no matter how good the laws you set up. the people in power would bend them to fit their own desires. He stated this out of frustration, it seems, with the way Pennsylvania turned out.

So I believe we rarely do good deeds because of demand or law, but usually because they are an outpouring of the good within us. And it is rarely because of pay: money is the lubricant of life, not the substance. Rather, spirit underlies all, and is where healing and growth and imagination begin.

In middle age, we recognize, one by one, the bad habits of youth. And we try to change them in order to live long and well. But the habits and addictions are often deeper then smoking, or eating too much, or procrastination. They may include avoiding the truth, or living too much in the past or future, or doing three things at once. They may include excessive anger, or pessimism, or avoiding relationships, or tolerating too much pressure for too long. Deep faults, becoming a quagmire.

In my case, the faults were many. Elitism, male chauvinism, cowardice in the face of controversy, some passive-aggressive tendency thrown in. My task is now to weed these out, refining myself spiritually for a happier maturity. Incidentally, in the process. I've come to accept my name. Whereas I earlier felt it demeaning, the person doing a common, manual task, I now recognize it as more worthy; I am a weeder of human gardens.

Leaving practice recently, I have the time and energy to weed myself of flaws, as I say. But the other side of my activities is spent in planting ideas into the receptive soil of those in distress. So you, my reader, are the recipient of this propagation. Illness is a good time for change, a "wake-up call." I hope the ideas prove nourishing to your spirit. I hope they make you aware, in the Buddha's sense, of what illness is, and how you may heal yourself. If I have left you with that, I am very grateful.

I have observed many deaths, in both young and old. You may have too. Some die suddenly, it is true, from heart attacks, strokes or accidents. But don't most of us leave this life slowly, inch by inch, as imperceptibly as weight loss, hair loss, memory failure? Until one day the person makes the seemingly undramatic decision not to take another in-breath?

And isn't what brings us to this moment equally undramatic? It may be the dragging weight of oft-repeated wrong choices or the smothering weight of sorrow. In primitive societies, it may be as mysterious as a voodoo curse. In our local community, it may be the loss of love, an angry glance. A broken heart can break. Physically strong—we can absorb enormous punishment, and labor under heavy yokes. But the spiritual web is a spider's, fragile, felt but not seen. It breaks and we fall, killed by a look or a hateful motive.

With cancer, the energy/spirit dwindling is often speeded up. Cancer is a draining open sore. But all "natural" death is ultimately a loss of energy to live, whether timely or not. All life and healing is, as Paul and Paracelsus agree, of the abundance of spirit.

The Quarrel at Independence Hall

My friend wanted to see where it had all started in Philadelphia. And, my forebears having had something to do with it, I felt competent to be her guide.

The Liberty Bell was first. Everyone doesn't know the story. The usual report equates the ringing bell with the announcement of freedom from English rule of 1776. False, the bell had been cast in 1750 to commemorate William Penn's proclamation in 1700 of "liberty throughout the land" to his colonists. It wasn't until 75 years later that its heart was broken to celebrate a war. The crack was repaired several times, I understand. But the original message rang out freedom of worship, freedom of assembly, freedom to live life according to one's conscience, not freedom from the British yoke.

Penn's Quaker message had always sounded to my ear like the Bill of Rights. Recently, I found out why. My Quaker namesake had been a lawyer. His law clerk, James Madison, had written the Bill of Rights before becoming our third president.

My friend and I waited in a long line before entering Independence Hall. The place, if you've seen it, is a plain squared room of about eighty simple desks and chairs. But what our young speaker revealed was far from plain. Eloquently for a non-orator, he described the open warfare that had occurred in those crucial days when eighty-odd men pledged their "lives, fortunes, and sacred honor," in the name of rebellious freedom. The British price for this traitory was hanging from the neck until dead. No less. Till dead, and the loss of all property.

But it was far from simple. The mercantile New Englanders defended their goods and trades. Their tradition had been different from what Penn had advocated. Their progenitors had been Puritan, allowing no deviation from their strict religiosity. Again, the penalty was hanging. Visiting Pennsylvania Quakers had found this out. But that was several years before. The John Adams family no longer felt that way, fortunately.

The forestry lecturer went on to describe the dignified mint-Julep southerners, cultivating cotton and tobacco with black men and women. And the dirt farmers of western plains, the fishermen of watery places, the Catholics in the middle. How were all these types, these varied industries, these warring faiths to agree on anything, let alone how to oppose a common tyrant?

With quarreling projected to a common aim, and mutual respect, merging of opinion was possible. "I may not agree with what he said, but I'll defend to the death his right to say it." I suppose good dinners together, lubricated with fine wine and Franklin's wit, may have had something to do with it when the time came for a vote. There were some hot heads, some bruised feeling, but very few came to a duel.

Tolerance is a Quaker virtue. "There is that of God in every man." What seems obvious today may appear very different tomorrow, when it's not raining.

The result of this confrontation in good will was a document balancing like a fine watch the interests of all, checks and balances which for three hundred years have prevented the domination of one societal group over another, all in the name of truthful cooperation. Nowadays, removing both truth and cooperation, we face chaos. Will our winning combination prevail? We'll see.

Missions of Healing

My mission began when my wife died. It was the undeniable, cruel, too immediate ending to what had been a comfortable, rather predictable series of episodes, passing month by month, year by year, toward what I thought would be my own finishing. It should have been years before the passing of my much younger wife, Areta. Her name, in Greek, meant 'highest virtue.' And with her talents she'd seemed destined for greatness. Then, suddenly, she was the sick one, her considerable beauty and celebrated vivaciousness giving way to a full years' aging each and every month to the wasting of an Egyptian mummy.

I fled to the water, from which I've always imagined my primeval ancestors rising. Within days of her death, I travelled to a marina at Tom's River, where I had previously seen some old but serviceable boats. One I'd noticed years before was still there. Didn't look like it had moved out of its slip for maybe four or five years. It had been made by Carver, a respected builder—with a name appropriate for an old surgeon. I felt confident that the hull, fiberglass, would be sound. The interior, through a window, looked like boat fixer-upper. Thirty two comfortable feet long, with most of the amenities for live-aboard existence. I figured the owner was tired of paying slip fees, and would bargain. I was right. My friend Giorgio and I spent weekends travelling to the shore getting it shipshape.

The boat and I went south, both on wheels. We met in Florida, where a crane lifted "Bel Canto" gently back into the water. Our nerves on edge, we filled the long-unused gas tanks with a toxic mixture of potions meant to soak up excess water, clean out debris, and increase octane to an explosive level. Holding our breaths, the captain and I lit the fuses, and the 250 horsepower Commanders roared into life like hungry lions. Wow! What a feeling of power! And at this point, I needed power.

But finding a boat-home was only the beginning of healing. I soon met Theresa, a woman too young for romance with me, but experienced and sensitive enough for a very solid and mutual friendship. Sort of adopted daughter, you might say, but filled with the fun and spice it's hard to have with someone who's grown up under your critical eye. We travelled to Hawaii together, where Theresa kindly helped me scatter Areta's ashes in the same sacred waters Areta and I, thirty years before, had spread her mother, Inez. True to the fun we share, Theresa and I also hiked the trails and saw the volcanoes those wonderful islands offer.

From rather different backgrounds, Theresa and I have bonded over medicine (she is a cardiac nurse), a concern for doing something for others, interests in travel, art, music, and sailing. Over some time, we have developed a healing, mutual respect, and care. One aspect of this was her early expressed desire to go on a medical mission. With my good luck, I found the answer in the form of my son-in-law's relative, Father Pat of Blessed Trinity.

The conclusion of my personal healing happened with our medical mission to Uganda. How would it be possible to continue feeling sorry for oneself, and one's lot in life, when confronted by the joyous faith and warm smiles of the African people? More than an inspiration, it was an existential accusation of self-centeredness. Under the influence of my heart-nurse, and surrounded by the beating rhythm and sweet lilt of their young song, my old, tired heart responded, "Yes."

Recovery

The painful, gruesome death of my beautiful, vivacious wife left me in a deep, dark hole. I left town, escaped to the warm weather, welcoming beaches, sunny smiles of Florida. I made some wonderful new friends of both genders, ones who loved laughter and loved to play in the sun and water. I tried out a couple of new Quaker meetings, and found peace and welcome in the one in Sarasota. I did some boating, something that had been denied me by Areta's motion sickness for the years of our marriage. One special friendship was particularly healing.

Then, about three months ago, I tried something altogether different. While finding myself waking several times each night, and usually bothered by music when trying to sleep, I decided to leave the radio on all the time, even during sleep. Blessed by the best good music (classic) station I'd ever heard, I tuned both my living room stereo and my tiny bedroom portable to the given wavelength, and left them there, the bedroom one on very low. The first thing I noticed was that, far from being bothered by the almost instinctive melodies at night, I would find myself being lullabyed for the first few hours, greeted by lovely sounds when wakened, and relullabyed for the next interval of rest.

Next, after a few weeks of this, I suddenly opened my computer one day and wrote! I hadn't had a thing to say since my wife's illness and demise. And the words flowed like they hadn't since my last book, twenty years ago. It was so easy, like telling funny stories to an old friend. For me, a very personal, very powerful, very healing miracle. That's the best way to describe it. What was going on?

For many years, I have been a strong advocate of meditation, practicing daily after returning from the existential horror of repairing half-dead wrecks from the killing fields of Vietnam. But meditation is, in a way, a little like masturbation. Nothing new, like a loving friend, is in the equation. I still think meditation is a great gift, providing calmness, introspection, a change of pace. But it is, nevertheless, home grown.

The difference was this. I was absorbing musical ideas nonstop, twenty-four hours a day. And they were great themes, from some of the finest minds that had ever lived, musical ideas of comfort, of beauty, of courage, of relationship. Thoughts without speech—all I needed to do was add the words to make arias!

Aphorisms

Religion and science are the yin and yang of the creation. And as far as religion strays from science is the extent of its irrelevance.

Money is the lubricant of life, not the substance.

A man need be stiff only twice—the second time is when he is dead.

Dishonesty is like landing a plane without seeing the ground.

Relationship is more important than money.

We own nothing, we are only renting.

The arts are the fruit and flower of the human spirit.

The most important things in life are what we leave behind.

The miracle of Jesus is neither in his virgin birth nor his resurrection but in his extraordinary life of wisdom and love.

Talk of miracles persuades one of the impossibility of holiness. The example of heroism, on the contrary, is contagious.

The spiritual power of Eastern practices linked to the scientific rigor of Western medical research is potent therapy.

The verbal restraint Quakers exercise in silent worship they oh so rarely exhibit in meeting for business.

War is the response of the small mind to the big problem.

Abstract art is visual music without words.

Nothing important is learned from those you agree with.

In most machines, oil and water are needed,
but they rarely make a good mixed drink.

The more extreme and powerful the art, the more it divides the critics. And what charms in youth may bore in maturity.

In the beauty of nature is healing of the human spirit.

A great disease is better than a war to bring the nation to its senses and rid us of flawed rulers.

The best answer to a bad quarrel is good sex.

I am constantly amazed at how much abuse blacks
will suffer, and still remain sweet-tempered.
Whites don't do it—they emigrate.

Good writing is like sharpening a blade, the
more you remove, the better the point.

The only person more stupid than a liar
is one who always believes him.

"Fool me once, shame on you. Fool me twice, shame on me."

It is a reasonable assumption that the same mechanisms
that improve immunity from cancer do so for coronavirus.

Do thank God for those who improve your reach.

Great writing is drawing lines of force
between ideas seemingly unrelated.

Get a dog: loyal, trainable, and they
will probably sleep with you.

Appendix

Medicine, Meditation and Osler's Aequanimitas

Medicine, Meditation, and Osler's Aequanimitas

Richard S. Weeder MD, FACS

Richard S. Weeder MD, FACS

Abstract

In this era of near-chaotic changing medical practice, it seems well to reflect on the past standard-bearers of our profession, our present state of mind and morale, and develop new emotional techniques and values suited to our challenges.

I hesitate to talk to fellow physicians about the philosophy of medicine as I am neither a philosopher nor a paragon. The things I will say will be more confession than counsel. And with this audience, I am addressing a group of colleagues who I respect as one of the best hospital staffs I have ever known. That said, I plan to share some thoughts about medicine and its future that have found their way into the butterfly net I hold up to the winds of change to furnish ideas for my jottings.

We are at a difficult time. The golden age of medicine is probably behind us, and may already have started to fade in the days of Osler, who is one of the subjects of this talk. The burdens of malpractice suits, of managed medical care, of excess competition, of decreasing pay, of increasing bureaucracy and heavy-handed oversight were not faced by Osler. And, indeed, they scarcely dimmed my father's optimistic smile fifty years later, in mid century. But they are now fully upon us, increasing in weight, and suffocating the joy that has previously suffused our glorious profession.

Again personally, I have not been immune to this negative shift. I too have been increasingly depressed by the transition from self-motivation to outside control by the unworthy, the materialistic, and the ill-informed. It has been so disheartening for me that, on two occasions, I fled the storms of practice for the calmer waters of teaching and writing. My sanity required it. Again, I am no paragon, as flawed as any. Yet perhaps my struggles can inform your struggles, my history can smooth your path.

I find my personal standards slipping. The other three surgeons in my family would be disappointed when I say, or even wish, that a troublesome patient would go away. I jokingly tell my nurse, "I'd like to think of her as your patient," when faced with such an irritant. But, truth be told, the winning over of such a crusty client can be a personal triumph of gratifying dimensions, and a lesson in our own imperfections.

Author
- Department of Surgery
Straub Clinic and Hospital
Honolulu, HI 96813

Correspondence to:
Richard S. Weeder MD, FACS
888 S. King St.
Honolulu, HI 96813
(808) 522-4397
Email: rweeder@straub.com

So how do we deal with all this. How do we develop the unperturbability and equanimity Sir William Osler so much valued in the seasoned physician? Let me set the stage by quoting from his famous address to the graduating medical school class of 1889 at The University of Pennsylvania.

> *"In the first place, in the physician or surgeon no quality takes rank with imperturbability...Imperturbability means coolness and presence of mind under all circumstances, calmness amid storm, clearness of judgment in moments of grave peril, immobility, impassiveness...In the second place, there is a mental equivalent to this bodily endowment, which is as important in our pilgrimage as imperturbability...-a calm equanimity is the desirable attitude. How difficult to attain, yet how necessary, in success as in failure!*
>
> *A distressing feature in the life which you are about to enter, a feature which will press hardly upon the finer spirits among you and ruffle their equanimity, is the uncertainty which pertains not alone to our science and art, but to the very hopes and fears which make us men. In seeking absolute truth we aim at the unattainable, and must be content with finding broken portions.... Engrossed late and soon in professional cares, getting and spending, you may so lay waste your powers that you may find, too late, with hearts given away, that there is no place in your habit-stricken souls for those gentler influences which make life worth living"*

There is much more quotable here, but let us take only this one inspiration, store it away, to revisit in a few moments.

I'd like to make one more quote, not exactly about equanimity, but about the attitude we might assume when faced with personal anguish and uncertainty. I was fortunate in college to have a religion professor who later became a close friend. His name was Malcolm Diamond, and he was one of the professors whose lecture halls were always filled. One day, when we were having lunch together, I asked him, among all the scriptures he knew by heart, what passage gave him most comfort when facing a crisis. He answered me, not from the Torah, the Koran, the Bible, or the Bagevad Gita, but from "Lord Jim," by Joseph Conrad. The passage is from the middle of the text, and is repeated with slight variation a few pages later. Stein is talking to Marlow, and both are in a philosophic frame of mind.

"A man that is born falls into a dream like a man who falls into the sea. If he tries to climb out, as inexperienced people endeavor to do, he drowns---nicht wahr...No! I tell you! The way is to the destructive element submit yourself; and with the exertions of your hands and feet in the water make the deep, deep sea keep you up."

The point of Conrad's metaphor, then, is to have an attitude that does not run away from problems, but rather enters them, works on them with knowledge, intelligence and courage. But let us now turn from an attitudinal point of view to a more physiological, anatomic, and practical approach to the mind and spirit.

Much has been learned about the mind in the past 100 years and its links to the endocrine and even the immune system. Herbert Benson at Harvard has proven the benefits of meditation in controlling, not only catecholamines and blood pressure, but brain waves themselves. Religion, or at least some religious practices, has thus become a legitimate bed-fellow of science. Einstein remarked that "Religion without Science is blind, but Science without Religion is lame." The practice of meditation has been mimicked by other stress-relieving techniques: the great Frank Leahy would frequently step back from the operating table, sit down with gloved hands before him, and meditate when faced with a surgical conundrum. I myself used to turn away and splash my hands in the scrub-bucket in times of surgical uncertainty, so much so that my scrub nurses would occasionally grace my bucket with a sterile rubber ducky!

Scientific investigation has shown that meditation, beside being a practice going back thousands of years and followed in nearly all known religions, can give more rest than sleep itself. And we find it provides sharper focus of the intellect and greater control over that ·ky monkey -mind that bends our attention to elephants when ˬ want to think of something else; that mental noise that repeats parental put-downs on endless tapes of the super-ego. It seems the older we get, the more our thoughts turn to past and future. And the more we need the living-in- the- moment which meditation provides. The newest proponent of this idea is Eckhart Tolle in his best selling, *"The Power of Now"*. Now is the only moment over which we have absolute control. The past has already slipped from our grasp, and is, for most of us, about eighty percent regret; the future becomes increasingly uncertain as we age, also about eighty percent anxiety. Joy is possible only in the NOW. Tolle has westernized this eastern wisdom represented by Thich Nat Hahn and Eknath Easwaren; Jon Kabat Zinn has put it into practice. As Jerry Jampolsky says, forgiveness is the greatest healer of all. And he quotes a patient: "forgiveness is giving up all hope for a better past." Now, once again, is the operative moment, the only one we can control, for better or worse.

This is not to assert that meditation can be practiced only by sitting quietly, eyes closed, in the lotus position with running water gurgling at your side. No, as the sage tells it, meditation can also be in chopping wood and carrying water. Or in making tea. Or in paddling a boat. Or in delighting in a glorious sunset. Or on hearing captivating music. Or in watching the glistening, marching waves. Or even in tracing the fine trajectory of a golf ball destined for an eagle putt. I used to calm when entering the operating room, knowing I had a completely absorbing task in front of me and no possibility of g disturbed while doing it. And as you golfers might agree, if you start to think of past or future on the golf course, you've blown the game.

So meditation, meditation of all sizes, varieties, origins, can be a superb stress-reliever, taking us miles from the petty and not-so-petty demands of our profession. I commend it to you.

And yet, we badly need more than stress-relief. In this time of rapid change and near-chaos, we also need standards, values, and motives that will stand up to this time and make possible a future with an ethos not superficially based on six-month accountant's figures. Our Western civilization has been shaken, not only by contact with a non-compliant middle East, but also by a challenging Rising Sun and a materialistic television-based life style. Our parochialism is Greek, or Latin, to our new neighbors and new kinsmen from around the world. So where is the moral Pole star that is True North from any ethical position on the globe?

I reconsider the values of my own Judeo-Christian tradition. They retain some validity for me, but I find them wanting as expressions of clear vision and "purity of heart," to use Kierkegaard's phrase. If we take the Ten Commandments, for example, and study them for relevance, we find most of them wanting. On a day by day basis, I'm not usually found coveting my neighbor's wife. At least not in my advancing age, wisdom, and satisfaction with my own marriage. Nor am I tempted to kill or steal – it's not fashionable. As far as honoring my father and mother, they've been dead for half my lifetime now. Or the golden rule, "do unto others." There are many times when I think ill of myself, when I put myself down. Should I do that also to my neighbor? Or how about self hate to the point of suicide. Is that justification for killing the other? Martin Buber stated truth here, with his "I and Thou." No. I find western civilization and philosophy lacking in what I choose to label "useful imperatives," or moral guides that are helpful day by day in our relations with family, friends, patients and colleagues.

The Buddha has provided four such "useful imperatives." They are known collectively as "The Four Sublime or Excellent States." And they are as follows;

Loving kindness

Shared Joy

Shared Sorrow

Equanimity

And here we revisit Osler's ideal! I don't know to what extent Sir William was a student of Eastern Philosophy, but it seems he was on the same path. With regard to the other three imperatives, Lovingkindness is certainly an attitude which any humanist understands and can embrace, as are Shared Joy, (rejoicing in the happiness of others) and Shared Sorrow, or empathy. I commend these excellent states to you as personal goals which cannot be misunderstood, misinterpreted, or faulted. They are truly Sublime, altogether worthy of our attention, whether in the twenty-first century practice of medicine or in the by-ways of life and family.

References

Conrad, Joseph. Lord Jim. New York: Dell Publishing Co., Inc. 1961

Easwaran, Eknath. Conquest of Mind. Tomales, Ca: Nilgiri Press. 1988

Jampolsky, Gerald G. Forgiveness : The Greatest Healer of All. Hillsboro, OR: Beyond Words Pub. 1999

Kierkegaard, Soren. Purity of Heart is to Will One Thing. Perseus. 1974

Nhat Hahn, Thich. The Miracle of Mindfulness. Boston: Beacon Press. 1975

Osler, Sir William. Aequanimitas. New York: Mcgraw-Hill, Blakiston Division

Tolle, Eckhart. Practicing the Power of Now. Novato, California: New World Library. 1999

Wallace, R.K. and Benson, H. The Physiology of Meditation. "Scientific American". Vol. 19:226 1972 pp.84-90 1972

New Hope for Cancer
A changing Paradigm

Good afternoon.

Last month, in *The New York Times,* the recent advances in the field of cancer were variously lauded by three prominent oncologists as "Amazing," "A game-changer," and "A watershed moment." One said, "This period will be viewed as an inflection point, a moment in medical history when everything changed." In the last fifty years or so, there have been major advances in many conditions, but as far as cancer is concerned, this is the most dramatic and significant progress of all. Accordingly, the survival figures are already reflecting these breakthroughs, running as high as 80% for some very dangerous tumors.

In the discouraging "war on cancer" announced by Nixon fifty years ago we have been using surgery, chemotherapy, and radiotherapy as the primary means of tumor removal. One might make the analogy that this approach is like the army, carrying out the same aim in three different ways. But we have now added to our forces immunotherapy and genetics, the "air force and navy, "so to speak. Neither of the latter removes tumor en bloc but rather strengthens the patients' defenses to deal with it on a cellular level. The first is like hitting the malignancy with a sledge hammer, the other removes it cell by cell, leaving surrounding tissues uninjured. Both techniques may be needed to properly treat the tumor, but there is no doubt that this combined approach is proving more effective and more easily tolerated. More about this later.

First, I am going to describe the characteristics of cancer, what makes it different from other illnesses. Then I will give some advice as to how best to mentally and emotionally confront the condition—what attitude should one take in dealing with it. Lastly, I will go into some detail describing the new paradigm and the modalities, both recent and older which can help provide remission. I use the term remission rather than cure, as recurrence is always possible. "Control" is an even better word to use when describing our efforts.

How does cancer work?

First of all, cancer has a multitude of causes and predisposing factors. It is well known that we are all fighting off cancer throughout our lifetimes, with an average of six "silent" cancers occurring in someone of retirement age. So why do only some become apparent and threaten our lives while others remain unobserved?

Predisposing factors for cancer development include chronic irritants, decreased immunity, genetic abnormalities, hormonal changes, stress, and loss of energy. Chronic irritants include inhaled particles such as cigarette smoke and asbestos. Excessive sunlight promotes cancer of the skin; fluctuating hormones may stimulate malignant changes in sex organs such as breast, prostate, uterus, cervix and ovaries. Various chemicals can affect the urinary bladder, and fatty acids from breakdown products of meat can initiate cancer in the large intestine. Apparently, what happens is that, as the tissues attempt to heal themselves from chronic damage, rapidly growing cells "de-differentiate" into out-of-control tumor cells. Recent work has illustrated that this damage occurs under the influence of genetic abnormalities, with alterations in the cellular DNA. Our exposure to chronic irritants is something under our control; one can avoid cigarette smoke, excessive sunlight, and toxic diets. Enough said.

Attitude

The first line of defense against cancer is the patient's attitude toward it. Now what is the best mind-set to adopt when confronted with malignancy?. Should one consider it a physical attack, like an auto accident or an attack by a mugger? Or should one lie back passively, as if getting a massage, and let doctors, nurses and family take charge? Or perhaps you should scurry about, trying this, trying that, indiscriminately expending time and energy? Should you call all your friends and neighbors to ask their advice? Should you go from one hospital or doctor to another, seeking the perfect medical advice? No, there is a better behavior model.

I was lucky to have as friend and mentor Professor Malcolm Diamond of the Religion Department of Princeton University. One day over lunch I asked him, in all his experience with the world's great scriptures, what passage gave him most comfort in times of trial. He replied, not from the Bible, the Torah, or the Tao Te Ching, but from the novel *Lord Jim*, by Joseph Conrad. The passage is as follows: Stein and Marlow are having a deep philosophical talk about life, and Stein remarks:

> *A man that is born falls into a dream like a man who falls into the sea. If he tries to climb out, as inexperienced people endeavor to do, he drowns*—nichi wahr... *No! I tell you! The way is to the destructive element submit yourself; and with the exertions of*

your hands and feet in the water make the deep, deep sea keep you up."

This seems to me the perfect metaphor for how to deal with cancer. Particularly for a swimmer somewhat afraid of the water, I appreciate the concept that one does not flail about but rather immerses oneself, gently but firmly stroking, and thus survives. The advice is to neither give up on the one extreme nor panic on the other. Find out as much as you can about cancer, and the specific treatment options for your type. Keeping your "cool," your equanimity, study dispassionately what confronts you. Enter the destructive, dangerous "element" fully prepared, head up. This attitude will greatly increase your chances of survival and, in the meantime, it will be rational and creative. Become a "swimmer of the deep." I have known many patients who bless their cancers for a valuable existential lesson it has taught them, no matter what the outcome.

The New Paradigm

Now how does one get rid of cancer? Until very recently, as noted above, the only accepted treatment involved the removal of the tumor by means of surgery, chemotherapy, and/or radiotherapy. These techniques lower the "tumor burden" by decreasing the size of the tumor. But within the past few months, two other factors have been discovered to be crucially important, the above mentioned immunity and genetic defects.

I became aware that tumor removal was not the whole answer to therapy while a medical student, working with C. Everett Koop. Dr. Koop, who was later surgeon general under

Reagan, had been dealing with the neuroblastoma, a malignant tumor in children which has the unusual propensity to frequently disappear after it has been only *partially* removed. This phenomenon, known as"spontaneous remission" has been witnessed in every other cancer known to medical science, though not as frequently as with neuroblastoma. The usual explanation for this has been for the physician to lamely call it "miraculous," or make some other fanciful attribution. But in the case of neuroblastoma, what apparently happens is that, with removal of part of the malignancy, the tumor burden is lowered enough so that the child's natural defenses are able to eradicate the remaining tumor tissue.

Two other clues to the existence of other unnamed healing factors are as follows: the phenomenon of delayed recurrence, where someone tumor-free for long periods suddenly has return of tumor and sudden death. And then there is the case of the heavy smoker who does *not* get cancer. Now, I'd like to ask the audience about these phenomena. May I have a show of hands of any who have witnessed a spontaneous remission, or "miracle cure." And how many of you have know people who seemed disease-free for many years, and then suddenly have recurrence and die after a difficult happening in their life? We all have witnessed the heavy smoker who seems immune to lung cancer.

These three phenomena are fully understood in the new light of immunity and genetics. Parenthetically, AIDS is such a devastating condition because it cripples the immune system, resulting in lowered resistance to both infections and malignancies.

An important aspect of malignancy is the energy drainage which it entails. Although hard to measure, our energy reserves are what make healing possible. In the face of great energy loss, or fatigue, the resistance to malignant overgrowth becomes markedly lowered. Other energy drains include the conventional use of surgery, chemotherapy, and radiotherapy.

Now practically speaking, all this leads us to a quandary: where does the physician draw the line between the positive effects of removing tumor burden and the negative effects of the energy drain which this entails? Answering this reveals the great advantage of immunology and genetics, as neither one is a significant energy drain. Both can be added to therapy without causing the damage done by conventional tumor removal. Moreover, there are many "complementary' or "alternative" modalities which are energy boosters, and therefore promote remission. These modalities are fully described in our little book *The Key to Cancer,* which I believe you have all been given. Parenthetically, and happily, all the suggestions made in the book have been ratified by the current advances we are describing today. And what is even more gratifying is that the five predictions made at the end of the book have all come to pass.

Briefly, these suggested modalities include nutrition, exercise, meditation, Yoga (including Tai Chi and Chi Gong), laughter, stress reduction, acupuncture, massage and attitudinal healing as practiced by Jerry Jampolski. Most of these techniques have been found to increase the immunologically active, anti cancer, T cells. And, parenthetically, T cell levels are decreased by stress and adrenalin, so stress reduction improves immunity. We have proven "the power of positive thinking," as described by Dr. Norman Vincent Peale so many years ago. The idea was remarkably far-sighted.

Lastly, we recognize the emotional or spiritual aspect of cancer. A healthy attitude may be described as will-to-live, optimism, motivation, or faith, call it what you will. But without it, all other therapy seems doomed to failure. As Soren Kierkegaard maintained, "Despair is the sickness unto death." And I can't resist the temptation to note that these advances combine elements of Western medicine with techniques developed over the ages from the East, a true yin and yang of therapy.

Expressed differently, I am reminded of the statement made by Franklin Delano Roosevelt in the dark days of the recession, "The only thing we have to fear is fear itself." This idea may be properly restated with regard to cancer, "The thing we have to fear the most is fear itself."

Now, how does this new use of genetics and immunology work? This is a highly complex process, beyond the scope of this paper. And there may be many alternate methods in carrying this out. But, simply stated, it is to take an autologous tumor cell lysate, genetically engineer it in tissue culture to attack a malignancy, and then reintroduce it to the patient, a veritable cancer "vaccine." Dr. Carl June at the University of Pennsylvania is leading the research into this process. It appears that the technique can be used for many different kinds of cancer. I've been told at a Penn meeting last month that genetic mapping to make the process more efficient is planned for the near future.

It is premature to claim that we have this all wrapped up, but we *can* claim that we understand the process much better than we used to, and we are discovering, day by day, much more rational and effective treatment. We are truly in a new era of cancer treatment.

So my advice to the patient includes several things. First, the patient should find an oncologist familiar with these new treatment techniques. Second, enlist the advice of a naturopath or other practitioner of complementary care to tailor for you the modalities which will enhance your *natural* defenses and immunity. (Parenthetically, this is the program now adopted at M.D. Anderson hospital, perhaps the leading cancer center in the world.) Then *you* should participate as a team member with all the therapists, making sure that they communicate with each other and with you. Lastly, adopt the swimmer's attitude of vigor, persistence, and hope, for you now have much more to be hopeful about. Do all the above in a timely manner, and you have contributed greatly to your survival.

Thank You and Aloha

The Educational Approach to Advanced Cancer

The Educational Approach to Advanced Cancer: A Preliminary Report

Richard S. Weeder MD, FACS, Ira Zunin MD, MPH, Ian Okazaki MD, and Fedor Lurie MD

Abstract

Survival from cancer depends primarily on reduction of tumor burden through surgery, chemotherapy, and radiotherapy. But other factors such as energy levels, immunity, and will to live have long been known to play a part. Some of these factors are best provided by complementary therapy. Our program, educational in nature, attempts to make these modalities available to the patient.

Thirty-odd years ago, President Nixon declared war on cancer. Our response has been to destroy tumor with the "heavy artillery" of surgery, chemotherapy and radiotherapy. But we have almost completely ignored the "infantry" of immunity enhancement, the "air force" of energy repletion, or the "navy" of hope and optimism, areas long recognized as important to survival. Bits and pieces of complementary care are being offered increasingly, but few if any cancer centers offer the entire array of tools that are available for increasing immunity, energy, and hope. We need to use complementary modalities with the same vigor and thought we do "conventional" medicine in order to provide the total care of which we are capable.

We have seen some victories in this war. Our knowledge of cellular and molecular mechanisms of cancerogenesis increases exponentially; new and more effective treatments emerge, and new diagnostic techniques help to detect tumors earlier. The major defeat, however, has become clear in the area of education: most patients either complement their treatment or even replace it with some "alternative" modalities.

Authors' Affiliations
- Straub Clinic and Hospital, Honolulu, HI 96813 (R.S.W., I.O.)
- The Straub Foundation, Honolulu, HI 96813 (F.L.)
- Manakai O Malama Integrative Healthcare Group, Honolulu, HI 96813 (I.Z.)
- Rehabilitation Center, Honolulu, HI 96817 (I.Z.)

The reasons are many. Scientific knowledge is dynamic by nature; what we presented as evidence-based yesterday may not be so today. Previous data that fruit and vegetable consumption is protective against cancer has been challenged (Van Gils, G.H. et al JAMA 2005; 293:183-193; Smith-Warner, S.A., et al. JAMA 2001: 285: 769-782). Thus sometimes the unchanging recommendations of alternative medicine seem more reliable than the shifting advices of "scientific" medicine.

Correspondence to:
Richard S. Weeder MD, FACS
P.O. Box 22897
Honolulu Hawaii 96823
Ph: (808) 923-3738
Email: dik1536789@aol.com

All of us with cancer experience have had patients who outlived our most optimistic projections, individuals who develop a new relationship, take up a vigorous exercise program, adopt a nutritious diet, "get religion" or whatever. We name these "remarkable recoveries," "spontaneous remissions," "miracle cures." And enough of these anecdotes laid end-to-end become clinical experience. But we don't need to posit divine intersession to explain them – simply an increase in energy stores, a maximization of immunity, the development of an optimistic attitude, or all three, and the scales are tipped toward survival (See figures 1 and 2).

Ignoring spiritual and psychological aspects of disease, and their healing power, is a shortcoming of existing cancer education programs. Several investigators have reported changes in death rates around holidays and birthdays suggesting that spiritual and social activities, and an optimistic attitude, can prolong survival. (Phillips, D.P., et al. Lancet. 1988: 2:728-732; Idler E.L., et al. AJS. 1992; 97: 1052-1079, Schofield, P., et al. Cancer:2004; 100: 1276-1282.). Although some studies question this relationship, (Young, D.C., et al. JAMA. 2004; 292:3012-3016), this important aspect has received little attention in the education, counseling and treatment of cancer patients.

One aspect of this area was recently recognized by the scientific community – the "placebo effect." The NIH has earmarked significant funds to investigate this phenomenon, known and used by physicians for centuries. Recent study showed that physicians and nurses still use placebos in treating patients and 94% of them found placebos generally or occasionally effective (Nitzan, U., Lichtenberg, P. BMJ 2004; 329: 944-946.)

It is with these factors in mind that we have organized, on the islands of Hawaii, a multicentric program of education in cancer. The program neither examines nor treats patients, leaving all treatment to the patients' oncologists. Patients are asked to check all changes in their health programs with their oncologists. And we attempt to keep in close touch with the oncologists with regard to the patients' progress. To repeat, we are an educational organization, not a cancer treatment center. Our reasons for staying educational are three – we don't want to interfere with established oncologist/patient relationships – we want to stay simple and focused on the information imparted – and we wish to make it easy for other groups to affiliate with us for the sake of quicker data collection and growth of the program.

Our faculties consist of practitioners from a broad array of disciplines which all contribute to one or more of the four factors of: tumor destruction, immunity, energy, and attitude. These teams usually include oncologists, exercise therapists, massage therapists, acupuncturists, naturopathic physicians, Yoga instructors, meditation teachers, and teachers of attitudinal healing. There is no doctrinal orientation, but student/patients are urged to get in touch with whatever religious resources may be important to them. Our teachers are well credentialed but chosen also for their ability to teach. And they instruct from a syllabus which assures uniformity in the information imparted from one "school" or program to the next.

In conjunction with the above, a clinical research study is being developed with the help of the University of Hawaii. This study will investigate our thesis that a patient well informed in complementary modalities for cancer treatment will outlive one not so exposed, and will have a better quality of life. It will measure the life expectancy figure predicted for each patient enrolled (from his or her oncologist) against his or her actual survival. Also utilized, as a double check, will be national survival figures for each tumor and stage. If the patients enrolled regularly exceed their predicted survival, this will prove our thesis.

We hope to enroll 300 subjects and develop an experience over three or more years. Multiple affiliated sites for the program will be involved, using our educational material and providing subjects for the clinical study. Cost per participant (patients, spouses, caregivers) runs in the $100 range for a two-day seminar.

A small pilot program was carried out six months ago (May, 2004) at the Straub Clinic and Hospital. Sample comments follow.

From Patients:

"Why didn't anyone else talk to us like this before."

"I am more aware of beneficial courses to take, thanks to you folks."

"A different spiritual approach, slowing down by getting myself out of the way – making priorities and not constant confusion."

From Oncologists:

"I feel course was very helpful to patient. She appeared to have a very firm understanding of the cancer process as it related to her condition. Understood rationale for treatment recommendations."

"More relaxed, calmer, more accepting and understanding of his diagnosis and condition. Less stressed."

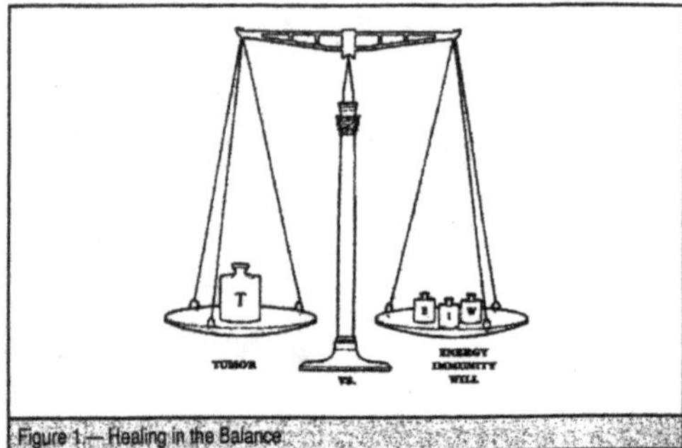

Figure 1.— Healing in the Balance

Panoramic Cancer Care					
	Less Tumor Burden	Immunity	Energy	Hope	Less Pain
EXERCISE	0	+	+	+	0
MASSAGE	0	+	+	+	0
ACUPUNCTURE	0	+	+	+	+
MEDITATION	0	+	+	+	+
CHEMOTHERAPYRADIO-THERAPY	++	Neg.	Neg.	+	?
SURGERY	++	Neg	Neg	+	?
NUTRITION	0	+	+	?	0
ANTIOXIDANTS	0	+	+	?	0
IMMUNITY	0	+	+	+	0
ATTITUDINAL HEALING	0	+	+	+	?
YOGA	0	+	+	+	?

Figure 2.— Treatment Modalities

Our program is also described on a web site, www.Alohacancereducation.org. Collaboration/affiliation is invited from other groups.

References

A Course in Miracles. Foundation for Inner Peace, Inc. 1975
Bock, Kenneth, and Sabin, Nellie. The Road To Immunity. New York: Pocket Books. 1997
Bovbjerg, D.H. and Valdimarsdottir, H.B. Psychoneuroimmunology: Implications for Psychooncology. In Holland, J.C. Psycho-oncology. Oxford: Oxford Univ. Press. 2001
Conrad, Joseph. Lord Jim. New York: Dell Publishing Co., Inc. 1961
Dickens, Charles. A Christmas Carol
Dossey, Larry. Healing Words. New York: Harper Collins. 1993
Dossey, Larry. What's Love Got To Do With It? In "Alternative Therapies" May 1996. Vol.2. No. 3
Easwaran, Eknath. Conquest of Mind. Tomales, CA: Nilgiri Press. 1988
Jampolsky, Gerald G. Forgiveness: The Greatest Healer of All Hillsboro OR Beyond Words Pub. 1999
Nhat Hahn, Thich. The Miracle of Mindfulness. Boston: Beacon Press. 1975
Ornish, Dean. Dr. Dean Ornish's Program for Reversing Heart Disease. NY Random House. 1990
Pelletier, Kenneth R. The Best Alternative Medicine. New York: Simon and Schuster. 2000
Reilly, David et al. Is Evidence for Homeopathy Reproducable? In "Lancet", Dec. 10, 1994 Vol. 344 pp.1601-1606
Seligman, Martin. E. P. Learned Optimism. New York: Pocket Books. 1990
Simonton, O. Carl, Mathews-Simonton, Stephanie, and Creighton, James L. Getting Well Again. New York: Bantam books. 1980
Specter, Michael. The Outlaw Doctor. In "The New Yorker," Feb. 5, 2001 (Article on Nicholas Gonzales, M.D.) pp.48-61.
Tolle, Eckhart. Practicing the Power of Now. Novato, California: New World Library. 1999
Wallace, R. K. and Benson, H. The Physiology of Meditation "Scientific American". Vol. 19: 226:1972 pp.84-90 1972
Weeder, Richard S. Surgeon. The View From Behind The Mask. Chicago: Contemporary Books. 1988
Weil, Andrew. Sound Body Sound Mind. Compact Disc. New York: Upaya, Division of Music. 1997
Weil, Andrew. Self Healing. Creating Natural Health for your Body and Mind. (Monthly Newsletter) Watertown, Mass.

A Letter

If This Be Treason

In contrast to Messrs. Morse '42 and Church '45 ["Letters," PAW, September 8], I am delighted that nearly half of the class of '82 say they would seek conscientious objector status if the draft were reinstated. I realize that these two gentlemen attended Princeton during a time when educational efforts were severely disrupted by the war. That may explain why they are so ignorant of the tradition of civil disobedience in the name of conscience which has been so important throughout our nation's history, and which motivated the immigration of many of our nation's first settlers. Perhaps if more Germans had objected for conscience's sake in the late '30s, the Princeton education of the '40s would not have been so disrupted.

As an Army Major during the Vietnam conflict, I am well aware of the mistakes of which our national policy is capable. I am sorry that, at the time, I did not have wisdom and courage enough to resist our nation's inappropriate demands. It is good that there are those who do. We need more who are motivated by the demands of their conscience and fewer motivated by national interest (greed) or national security (paranoia). As John F. Kennedy said, "War will exist until that distant day when the conscientious objector enjoys the same reputation and prestige that the warrior does today" (from Schlesinger's *Thousand Days*).

DR. RICHARD S. WEEDER '58

Princeton, N.J.

PRINCETON ALUMNI WEEKLY (ISSN 0149-9270)
VOL. 83, No. 4, October 20, 1982.
Published twice monthly September through May and once in June and July by Princeton University Press, 41 William St., Princeton, N.J. 08540.
Annual subscription $15.00 (foreign postage $5.00 extra); single copies $1.00.
All orders must be paid in advance.

Science and Religion in the Twenty-First Century

Religion without science is blind;
Science without religion is lame.
Einstein

The adherents of science and religion have clashed since the beginning of history, and never more than in our present era, threatening to drive our world into chaos. Yet a close examination reveals the remarkable similarity between the world-class, creative scientist and the truly holy of whatever sect. It is only the misinformed, immature second-rate thinkers of each camp that get us into conflict. Both disciplines explore the same creation and human existence. Like two pilgrims leaving from opposite sides of the earth, their footsteps are at angles, but lead to the same true North. And thus they meet at the top.

The Bundle of Individual Truth

The world shrinks, day by day; science and religion are yin and yang, a sinuous line cleaving it together rather than cleaving apart. The Latin origin of the word religion, to gather together sheaves of wheat and bind them up; means to bring together the experiences of life into a meaningful bundle. It follows that each young person's bundle is relatively unique. As Hamlet says to Horatio, "There are more things in heaven and earth, Horatio, than are dreamt of in your philosophy." That is why we choose our warriors from among the physically mature, not spiritually mature. But if we all lived 150 years and kept collecting sheaves, our bundles would be very much alike and war ridiculous. War is the response of the small mind to the big problem.

As Thomas Merton says, "Prayer is to religion as original research is to science." So the impulses of religion and of science are similar, differing only in the fact that each scientist must *prove* his bundle to his colleagues. Moreover, the scientific community comes down hard on the cheating scientist, but the errant preacher is disciplined, if at all, only by the I.R.S. or the courts, not by his colleagues.

The ultimate authority, if religion and science quarrel, must rest with science. Science is both universal, from East to West, North to South, and it is provable. Religion is neither.

The concept of a creator arises in both camps. It is less often stressed by the scientist because un-provable. To the religious-minded, of course, the idea is usually central, Buddhism being one of the exceptions. But in the original Judeo-Christian conception, God was similarly un-provable. The passage in Exodus is clear: "Who shall I say that thou art," asks Moses. The answer comes back, "I am that I am," or, differently translated, "My name is nameless." Thomas Aquinas tried, centuries ago, to prove the existence of God. His arguments ended pretty much where they began. God is unknowable, of a different order of being than humans, as foreign to our comprehension as calculus is to a dog. In Taoism, the same thought is expressed, "What is called the Tao is not Tao; what is called not-Tao is the Tao." For the careful theologian, the creator is the "*mysteriam tremendum*," in the words of Rudolph Bultmann.

The frequent conceit is that the scientist does not believe in God. That has not been my experience with first-rate, creative scientists. Einstein's quote above sets the stage. I never knew him, but Ray Male, the long-time mayor of Princeton, New Jersey, told me of Einstein's interest in religion. One day Male got a call from Einstein to the effect, "What are you Quakers doing with that old meeting house on Mercer Street?" (Einstein was fond of walking in the woods which border the meeting house.) "I <u>think</u> you should get it going again." Which Mayor Male and others did. Another day Einstein went through the Princeton phone book, picking out all the Jewish names, calling every one himself. His idea was to set up a Jewish center, which has since become another of the important religious groups in the town.

I've personally known three other world class scientists; two Nobel Laureate Physicists, two Princeton deans (one was both), all of whom had or have active affiliations with various churches. And they describe their prize-winning ideas in terms of inspiration, more art than deduction, coming from they know not where. One, Eugene Wigner, told me his most original ideas came to him during long walks in the woods—the same woods, incidentally, that Einstein trod.

Since the days of Copernicus and Galileo, religion and science have been at odds. But it seems that the religious have been more willing to adopt unholy means to impose their views than the scientist, who generally sits back and lets time prove his case.

The Devil of Dogma

For a young, inquiring mind entering a church, it should not be necessary to check his or her common sense at the door. Yet, from an historical perspective, the Catholic church invented Hollywood before Hollywood. Fantastic tales abound, miracles by the dozen, a Holy family to replace the one you might have missed, idols in every niche. The abuses Luther railed against still flourish. For the price of a Sunday contribution, a murderous Godfather is still absolved from six weekdays of crime. How many altar boys need have their lives ruined to remove one lecherous Monseigneur from his pulpit? Virgin Birth, Papal infallibility, excommunication for deviation from dogma are still proclaimed from Rome. What, pray tell, have these to do with the power, truth, and loveliness of Jesus' message? The only miracles I acknowledge are those of the spirit, where evil men and women become good, good become great: Moses and Mandela, Paul and Mohammed, Augustine, Joan of Arc, Ghandi, Malcolm X, and Martin Luther King. I often think the truly repentant criminal the holiest among us. Physical miracles seem both unbelievable and irrelevant, contrary to the laws of science and creation, rather produced to enhance the selling of a religious sect. So much so that the ship of the church has become so encrusted with barnacles of miracles, dogmas, and rites to render it dead in the water. Moreover, the typical Catholic church is a museum of idols, many of them great art, but worshiped as idols nonetheless.

The church, like Hollywood, reinforces our habit of suspending disbelief, attracting adherents with magic and unreality. "My religion is better than yours because it has, not one hero, but a gathering of saints." Numerous converts produce both money and political power—the business side of the Church since the time of Peter. But as Jesus recognized, there is nothing heavenly about earthly power. And I think he would agree that money is the lubricant of life, not the substance. "Lay not up for yourselves treasure on earth…"

Now we all need our icons, physical reminders of spiritual matters. From the rabbit foot to a cross, a lovely icon, worry beads and rosaries, a prayer or mantra—these are useful reminders to our wayward minds. But we lose the point when we take them for the real thing rather than for what they represent, and we end up overvaluing things. And so it is with sacraments.

The Silliness of Sacraments

Sacraments are a diversion from the real business of religion, which is to make spiritual and moral sense of our world. If one wishes to signify one's relation to a church by baptism, confirmation, marriage in and by the church, and some recognition of a life well lived, I see little harm. But I take communion to be stretching the point. To posit that one is actually partaking of the body and blood of Jesus seems a desire to flavor one's spiritual stew with a dash of cannibalism. Anthropologists tell us that the cannibal usually ate his enemy not so much to satisfy hunger as to absorb his spiritual powers, or *mana.* But to insist at mass that transubstantiation as actual is enough to send a scientist screaming in laughter from the sanctuary! Would that it were so easy, that a priest could indeed turn wine into blood and bread into flesh. With an incantation, we could prime our heart-lung machines with Gallo '98 and cover our severe bums with communion wafers.

And, again, what have these, pray tell, to do with the power, truth and loveliness of Jesus' message?

The Folly of Fundamentalism

I define the fundamentalist as one who, using distorted holy writ as a cudgel, attempts to control the lives of others, meanwhile believing he has learned all that life can teach him, which is probably true. And we have recently been pushed around by fundamentalists of both Islamic and Christian stripe. Their arrogant tunnel vision has killed a love that could have developed between brother and sister faiths and cultures, both of whom worship the same deity. On the Christian side, we have resurrected the Puritans of New England, our only forebears who tortured and hung dissenters. And their narrow-mindedness is still infesting our nation, stuffing out the flames of liberty our forefathers so hopefully lit in 1776.

We have lost a great opportunity to enrich our society with the many beauties of Islamic art, music, architecture and tradition. And the Islamic fundamentalists have lost great opportunity to avail themselves of modem commerce, creature comforts, education and political science. With Mercutio I say, "A plague o' both your houses."

The Sins of Salvation

The doctrine of salvation I find to be the most pernicious of all. First of all, there is nothing provable about it—no holy stamp, like a star of David, that validates the "saved." No color of skin, degree of education, accent of tongue, color of clothing, background of race, expression of face, smudge on forehead or dangling cross distinguishes the truly holy from the pretender. I often worry that those who call themselves born again aren't dead again. And the confrontation between the "Master Race" and the Chosen People" was disastrous for both, big time. On the other hand, many are stamped "infidels" and heathen only by their dress or accent.

Not only is this idea at the heart of much warfare and human misery, it is spiritually crippling to the individual. It results in complacency, elitism, and irresponsibility that resists personal improvement and spiritual maturation. One has 'retired' from the obligation to grow this part of our being, which is, indeed, the only growth area possible for the older among us. In other words, rather than sources of wisdom and insight, seniors might as well only prepare for death.

Salvation is crucial to fundamentalism, leading to separation of religion from religion and individual from individual. It is both intolerant and uncurious. And it always seems that those most concerned about salvation are those whose flaws put them most in need of it.

If one wishes to imagine a heaven, or posit that spirit undergoes reincarnation, I have no great quarrel. Like matter and energy, it seems reasonable to think spirit neither created nor destroyed. The idea gives comfort against the unthinkableness for many of life ending in a void, or creation without a creator.

In Sum

If God does exist, He (She or It) is unknowable to finite minds. Any attempt at description is blasphemy. Both science and religion seem to point, like compasses, toward an unseen creative force. But for science and religion to exist in harmony, indeed, to preserve our planet and our civilization, we must rid ourselves of the doctrines, sacraments and fantasies which encrust our faiths. On the other hand, our most effective means of saving souls, Alcoholics Anonymous and its brother organizations, have always acknowledged a Higher Power. Mankind has an undeniable yearning for the divine, but many settle for a heavily controlling, "politically aware," church and/or a book filled with both pearls and ambiguities. The impulse for relationship with the creator may be seduced by promise of heavenly rewards, or 72 dark-eyed virgins for the Islamic. But our shrinking world can no longer afford the absurdities of influence-hungry theologians and wild-eyed zealots. For as far as religion strays from science is the extent of its danger and/or irrelevance.

Curriculum Vitae

Curriculum vitae for...	Richard S. Weeder, M.D.	
Date of Birth	Sept. 2, 1936	
Place of Birth	Philadelphia, Pa.	
Marital Status	Married Areta Parle 1987 two children born 1965 & 1974 from previous marriage	
Church affil.	Society of Friends (Quaker)	
Height & WT.	5'10" - 175 Pounds	
Languages	French	
Education	B.A. Degree-	Princeton University, Princeton N.J. June, 1958
	M.D. Degree-	University of Penna., School of Medicine Philadelphia, Pa. May 1962
Specialty Certification	Surgery Dr. Weeder is a Diplomate of the American Board of Surgery, certified in February, 1969	
Licenses:	Pennsylvania, by examination, 1962 New Jersey, 1969 Hawaii, by examination, 1994	
Other interests	Writing, music, religion, education	
Medical Soc.	Fellow, American College of Surgeons Member, Medical Society of New Jersey Hawaii Society of Clinical Oncology Hawaii State Consortium for Integrative Health Care	
Military Status	Completed tour of Duty, U.S. Army, 1969, rank of Major	

Papers	As author or Co-author only Weeder, R. S.: A New Hypothermia Unit for the Control of Bleeding. Bull. Geisinger Medical Center 18: 51 1966 Gerow, F.J. and Weeder, R. S.: Fluid Silicone Continuous Immersion in the Treatment of Burns. Bull. Geisinger Med. Center 16:17 1964 Gerow, F. J. and Weeder, R. S.: Medical Aspects of the Treatment of the Burned Patient. Medical Clinics of North America 48: 1557, 1964 Weeder, R. S., Brooks, H. W. and Boyer, A.S.: Silicone Immersion in the Care of Burns. Plastic and Reconstructive Surgery, March 1967 39: 256-262 Weeder, R. S., Klinger, H.M., Collins, J.A., and Cahill, T.J.: Simplified Hypothermia for Gastrointestinal Hemorrhage: Current Experience with a New Apparatus. Pennsylvania Medicine 70: 61 Dec. 1967 Weeder, R.S., Bashant, G.H., and Muir, R.W.: Acute Noncalculous Cholecystitis Associated with Severe Injury. The American Journal of Surgery: 729-732 June 1970 Weeder, R.S., Medicine, Meditation, and Osier's Aequanimitas. Hawaii Med Journal, Vol. 63, June 1004 Weeder, R.S., Zunin, I, Okazaki, I, and Lurie, F.: The Educational approach to Advanced Cancer: A Preliminary Report. Hawaii Med Journal, Vol. 64, November 2005
Training and Experience (Medical)	Rotating Intern - Germantown Dispensary and Hospital, Phila., Pa. July 1962-June 1963 Resident in Surgery - Geisinger Medical Center, Danville, Pa. July 1963-June 1967 Staff, General Surgery - 249th General Hospital (1000 beds) APO San Francisco 96267 - under Norman Scott, Col., M.C. September 1967-August 1969 Associate, Dept. of Surgery Hunterdon Medical Center, Flemington, N. J. 1969-1970

Assistant Director. Dept. of Surgery H.M.C. 1970–1976

Director. Division of General Surgery H.M.C. 1976–1980, 1996–2001

Attending, Dept of Surgery H.M.C. 1969–89, 1992–2001

Courtesy Staff. H.M.C. 1989–1992

Assistant Clinical Professor of Surgery College of Medicine and Dentistry of New Jersey (Rutgers Medical School) 1972–1980

President. Hunterdon County Medical Society 1977

Active Staff, Straub Clinic and Hospital, Honolulu, Hawaii, Sept., 2001–Feb, 2004
Emeritus Staff, Feb. 2004–

Active Staff, The Queen's Medical Center, Honolulu, Hawaii, Sept.-Dec. 2005

Founder, Aloha Cancer Education Institute, May, 2004

(As Writer) Bread Loaf Writer's Conference, Middlebury College, August, 1983

Physician-writer's Conference, University of Connecticut at Farmington April 1984

Princeton Writer's Group, 1983

New School for Social Research, 1986–88
Courses under Sidney Offit, Richard Brickner, Hayes Jacobs, and David Weir

Published Surgeon: The View from Behind the Mask Contemporary Books, published June, 1988
Paperback ed. Berkley Books, March 1991

Published The Key to Cancer with nine co-authors, Hoaloha Books, April 2006

Community Interests:	Member. Board of Trustees, Princeton Day School, 1981-1984
	Member, Board of Trustees, Young Audiences of New Jersey, 1982-1987 Vice Chairman, 1983-1984
	Clerk, Quakertown Friends Meeting, 1975-1976
	Overseer, Princeton Friends Meeting, 1984-87, 1990-1993
	President (Clerk), Board of Trustees, Princeton Friends School, 1986-89 Member, 1986-1990
	Member, Board of Trustees, Princeton Friends Meeting, 1989-1992, 1999-2002 President, 1990-1991
	Member, Committee on Human Studies, (Institution Review Board), University of Hawaii 2004-2006
	Member, Hawaii Society of Clinical Oncologists. 2005-
	Member, Palliation Workgroup, New Jersey State Comprehensive Cancer Control Plan. 2008-.

To contact us or buy more books by Dr. Weeder

www.richardweeder.com

or

shop@richardweeder.com